YOUNG ATHLETES' ULTIMATE GUIDE TO MENTAL TOUGHNESS

TURN FAILURE INTO FUEL, LOSS INTO VICTORY, AND SETBACKS INTO COMEBACKS. 5 SIMPLE STEPS TO BUILD RESILIENCE, CONFIDENCE, AND GRIT IN SPORTS AND LIFE

CHAD METCALF

FOREWORD BY
CLAY BUCHHOLZ

MENTAL TOUGHNESS
AND CONFIDENCE

CONTENTS

COPYRIGHT © 2023 BY CHAD METCALF

Published by Studio 5326 LLC, United States of America.

Free Bonus Chapter - You will love this hack!

RESOURCES TO HELP YOU IMPLEMENT THE SYSTEM NOW

The first step is often the hardest when learning something new. That's why I have created these accompanying resources. They are laid out to follow the book. I recommend starting with the workbook as you read this book. Once the workbook is completed you will you will start your journal (there is an intro to journaling in the workbook).

FORWARD

MENTAL TOUGHNESS
AND CONFIDENCE

BY CLAY BUCHHOLZ

"You don't have to like losing, but you are going to have to learn how to accept it."

SKIP BUCHHOLZ

Mental toughness is something that you can use to your advantage in a lot of different ways. I found out very quickly through the ranks of professional baseball that ability only takes you so far. Being the best at a young age is something that can launch you to the highest of highs but can also drag you down to the lowest of lows if you don't have the right mindset.

If you play long enough, you are 100 percent going to fail. Being blessed with athletic ability is something not everyone is given, and a lot of athletes blessed with the "ability" have never failed. Failure is a word that most people in the sports world hate, especially if you've never failed before. The ability to use failure to your advantage is KEY. A quote my dad told me growing up is, "You don't have to like losing, but you are going to have to learn how to accept it."

I really didn't know what my dad meant for a long time until I tasted failure at the highest level of baseball. I was about five years into my professional career, and when I failed, I would put pressure on myself for the next four days (in between starts) to not fail the next time. All that did was add stress, making it a bit tougher for each start, one after the other.

I eventually concluded that just because the outcome wasn't what I wanted, it didn't mean I couldn't learn from it. I learned that failure could actually help me in many ways. Even in failure, there is always SOMETHING good that happened that I could take away from it. Feeling sorry for yourself isn't going to make you better. Figuring out what you did well will boost your mindset and confidence, allowing you to learn from your mistakes. When I had a rough game and things obviously didn't go my way, I used the 24-hour rule. The 24-hour rule allowed me to be mad at the outcome for the next 24 hours, and after that, it was over, and it was time to start my preparation for my next outing. The next day I would watch the game on video and figure out what I did well. This mindset shift allowed me to always take something positive from bad results. This shift was one of my focal points for understanding mental toughness.

Remember, you don't have to like losing, but you are going to have to learn to accept it. You do this first by moving past it (the 24-hour rule). Second, find something positive and build on it. To be great, you must learn to use failure to your advantage. Failure is inevitable; only those who learn to push through will reach the highest levels.

Clay Buchholz

2x World Series Champion

2x American League All-Star

INTRODUCTION

MENTAL TOUGHNESS
AND CONFIDENCE

I have always enjoyed watching my sons compete. My oldest son Maverick has always been a gifted athlete who was very good at whatever sport he played. These include baseball, football, and the martial arts of Brazilian Jiu-Jitsu (BJJ) and Judo. By age 7, he was the two-time Virginia Judo Open champion.

When he was about 13, I moved him from the kids' class in BJJ, which was not challenging for him, to the adult class. He went from dominating to being dominated. His confidence faded, and I could see his motivation also waning. What he had once loved, he was starting to hate. I started noticing changes in his attitude. Was it the pressure to perform? Had he developed a fear of failure? Or was it something deeper and more complex—an opportunity to build his mental toughness?

As a parent, coach, or young athlete, you must have witnessed the pressure that young athletes face in today's competitive sports environment. Perhaps you've seen young athletes who once loved their sport lose interest, quit, or burn out due to the overpowering pressure to perform. Or you've seen young athletes struggle with competition's mental and emotional demands, holding them back from reaching their full potential.

As I researched deeper into this issue, I discovered a shocking truth. A study by the National Alliance for Youth Sports showed that, of the 40 million youths participating in organized sports each year, 70 percent quit by age 13. This means most young athletes who start playing sports competitively eventually drop out, but why is this happening?

You probably know the challenges of staying motivated and engaged in competitive sports all too well. You've likely seen the frustration and disappointment when one loses interest or drops out altogether. Maybe you've even experienced it firsthand.

Picture a young athlete stepping up to the starting line, heart racing, palms sweating, mind consumed with doubt and fear. The pressure is overwhelming, and the thought of failure looms large. And then it happens—the young star athletes fail to perform. Why does this happen?

Surely it's not their lack of physical ability or talent for the game. Is it related to their mental capacity to cope with failure and challenges? Is it mental toughness that they lack? Many wonder if mental toughness is inherent in some people or can be gained through training.

What if there were ways to develop the mental toughness needed to overcome these challenges and perform at your best, even under pressure? There are ways to build mental toughness. When my son's confidence and motivation faded, I knew this was the perfect opportunity to build resilience. With a challenge, you can build mental strength. How do you get stronger in the gym? Obviously, you lift heavier weights. The mind is the same. It gets stronger by persevering through difficulty; the more challenges you overcome, the stronger your mental toughness will be. So, do the hard stuff.

As a former Navy SEAL, I know how to face and overcome obstacles. When I went to Basic Underwater Demolition school (BUD/s), I was 135 pounds, had never run further than a mile and a half, and had never been in the ocean. There were Olympic-caliber athletes there with me, and in the back of my mind I was thinking, "How am I going to compete with these guys?" By the end of BUD/s, I was winning the 4-mile timed runs. This happened for three main reasons. First, I wanted it badly. Second, I improved my skills; I got stronger and faster. Third, everyone faster than me quit during "Hell Week."

I know that building mental toughness isn't easy. It starts with the right motivation, disciplined consistency, and a plan to push beyond your limits. Motivation gets you started; discipline is what keeps you going when you're not motivated. I have faced countless challenges and setbacks in the military, in sports and in my personal life, and I know what it takes to overcome them.

But the truth is I didn't always have the knowledge and tools needed to build resilient mental toughness. I had to learn through trial and error, training and experience, and with the guidance of mentors and trainers who taught me the skills and strategies I needed to succeed.

I needed a book or a training guide to help with the all-too-common problem of young athletes quitting sports for this reason, but no suitable book was in sight. So, I wrote one myself. This is the book I asked my kids to read.

I wrote this book to share the knowledge and tools I have acquired over the years so that you can avoid the same mistakes I made and achieve your goals faster and more efficiently. I know what it's like to struggle with fear, doubt and anxiety, to feel overwhelmed by pressure, and to doubt your ability to succeed. But, I also know what it's like to overcome those challenges and emerge stronger, more resilient and more confident than ever.

If you're a parent, coach, or young athlete, take action with what you learn in this book and use the mental toughness techniques to help you overcome obstacles, push through adversity, and achieve your goals. As someone who has personally experienced the power of these techniques, I can say without a doubt that they are truly life-changing.

With the help of this book, you will become mentally tough, resilient, and unstoppable. You will learn how to bounce back from setbacks, overcome obstacles, and turn failures into opportunities for growth. You will develop the skills and strategies to handle pressure, stay focused, and perform at your best when it matters most. And as a result, you will achieve greater success in sports and life, reaching heights of personal and professional excellence that you never thought possible.

As you dive deeper into this book, you will discover nuggets of wisdom and specific tools that will help you build unbreakable mental toughness. You will learn to overcome fear, doubt, and anxiety and develop a mindset that empowers you to perform at your best, even under the most challenging circumstances. You will discover how to set and achieve goals, build self-confidence, and develop a growth mindset to help you thrive in sports and life.

Mental toughness is a critical trait that athletes must possess to achieve their goals and overcome challenges. It is the ability to remain resilient, focused, and determined despite adversity or setbacks. Having mental toughness can be the difference between achieving and not achieving your goals.

Many great athletes had to fight adversity to become what they are today. We have examples of Tom Brady, Michael Phelps, and Serena Williams, who have demonstrated exceptional mental toughness in their respective sports. Brady has won seven Super Bowl championships and has been considered an underdog throughout his career. His unwavering focus, determination, and work ethic have made him one of the greatest quarterbacks in history.

Phelps, the most decorated Olympic athlete of all time, who won 28 Olympic medals, (23 of which were gold) had to overcome significant personal and mental health challenges to achieve unprecedented success in swimming. He constantly pushed himself to overcome obstacles and reach new levels of achievement.

Serena Williams won 23 Grand Slam singles titles, more than any other woman or man has won in tennis in modern times. She has demonstrated a remarkable ability to maintain her competitive edge and mental strength.

This book is grounded in scientific research and real-world experience, making it more than just another self-help book. You'll learn what mental toughness is and why it's crucial for athletes. You'll discover how to set goals and create a plan for achieving them, stay focused and avoid distractions, stay confident and believe in yourself, and deal with setbacks and adversity. You'll also learn how to stay motivated and avoid burnout, how to develop two mindsets, how to embrace challenges, and how improving your physical skills will build your mental ones.

If you are ready to take your mental toughness to the next level and unlock your true potential as an athlete and person, this book is for you. With the insights, strategies, and exercises I share in this book, you will have everything you need to overcome obstacles, face your fears, and become the best version of yourself. You will learn from my experiences and the experiences of other successful athletes to gain the knowledge and tools you need to take your mental toughness to the next level.

CHAPTER 1
A SUPERPOWER

MENTAL TOUGHNESS
AND CONFIDENCE

"It's not the will to win that matters—everyone has that. It's the will to prepare to win that matters." — Bear Bryant

---

An Olympic-level 100-meter sprint is over in less than 10 seconds. There is hardly any time to think about it; the sprinter runs by instinct. The world sees the 10-second race, but they don't see the years of preparation and training. Becoming an elite athlete requires considerable sweat, training, practice, and hard work. Not everyone with talent and physical ability can sustain the years of effort needed to succeed. Why is it that some athletes accomplish their goals while others fail? Trainers have studied this question and found that of the many elements that make an athlete elite, the most important one is mental toughness. Hard work beats talent when talent doesn't work hard.

Bear Bryant was an American college football coach widely regarded as one of the greatest coaches in history. Bryant spent over 38 years as a head coach, including 25 years at the University of Alabama, where he led the team to 6 national championships, 13 conference championships and 24 bowl games. He also coached at the University of Maryland, the University of Kentucky, and Texas A&M University.

Bryant was known for his strict, no-nonsense approach to coaching and his emphasis on discipline, hard work, and team unity. He was a strong proponent of mental toughness and believed it was a key component of success in football and in life. He often stressed the importance of discipline, hard work and mental toughness to his players, and he was known for pushing them to their physical and mental limits.

Bryant believed that mental toughness was essential for success on the football field, because the sport requires players to perform under pressure, persevere through adversity, and make quick decisions in high-stress situations. He believed mental toughness was developed through practice, experience, and a strong work ethic. He often pushed his players to develop this quality through grueling workouts and intense practices.

Mental toughness is the ability to push through challenges, setbacks, and doubts in self-confidence and resilience. It involves focus, determination, adaptability and emotional control.

Mental toughness lets you persevere through challenging situations while maintaining focus, determination, and resilience. It involves having a strong mindset and the ability to handle stress, pressure, and adversity without losing confidence or becoming overwhelmed.

Mentally tough individuals can stay calm, composed, and focused in the face of challenges or obstacles, and bounce back from setbacks and failures. They can adapt to change, remain optimistic, and maintain a strong sense of purpose and motivation, even when faced with adversity.

Mental toughness is crucial because it helps you stay focused on the task and manage your emotions. It allows you to push through on bad days and stay focused on good ones.

Mental toughness is essential for young athletes. It's not just about having the ability to deal with the stress of competition, but also how they can handle their emotions during and after matches.

According to Professor Peter Clough, a pioneer in research into Mental Toughness, a mentally tough person is confident, resilient, and adaptable. They can handle challenges and difficulties, and they enjoy overcoming obstacles. Being mentally tough isn't insensitive or selfish; it's about having determination and confidence to persevere even when faced with difficult circumstances. It involves being comfortable with oneself and believing one can succeed despite adversity.

Angela Duckworth is a renowned psychologist. She authored a popular book, <u>Grit: The Power of Passion and Perseverance</u>. In this book, Duckworth discusses her research on the concept of "grit," which she defines as a combination of passion and perseverance toward long-term goals. In the book, she shares her findings from studying high achievers in fields such as sports, business and the military.

Through her research at West Point, Duckworth focused on measuring the level of mental toughness or "grit" among cadets and how it correlated with their success in completing the rigorous military training program at the United States Military Academy.

She chose 1,200 cadets undergoing their first summer of training, asking them to rate themselves on a scale of one to five on their perseverance, passion for long-term goals and ability to bounce back from setbacks.

Over the next two years, Duckworth tracked the cadets' performance and found that those who scored higher on the grit survey were more likely to make it through the grueling training program and become commissioned officers in the Army, while others who seemed physically stronger and tougher often did not.

This research validated the concept of "grit" as an essential factor in success, not just in military training but also in most other challenging pursuits. What was particularly interesting about what Duckworth concluded is that grit is a better predictor of success than other factors traditionally associated with achievements, such as intelligence or talent.

COMMON CHARACTERISTICS OF MENTALLY TOUGH PEOPLE

Mentally tough people have many common characteristics. Here are a few of them:

They don't fear taking calculated risks.

"Only those who will risk going too far can possibly find out how far one can go."

— T. S. Eliot

Mentally tough people do not shy away from taking calculated risks, even if it means stepping out of their comfort zone and facing potential setbacks. They meticulously weigh the pros and cons before making any significant decision and are fully aware of the consequences that may follow. To them, failure is just another obstacle to overcome. They understand that taking risks and pushing beyond their limits is necessary to achieve greatness. They are not reckless fools living in some fantasy world but rather are daring and bold, ready to venture into the unknown and face whatever challenges may arise. Their unwavering determination and willingness to take calculated risks set them apart, enabling them to reach new heights of success in all areas of their lives.

They take responsibility and hold themselves accountable.

"You cannot escape the responsibility of tomorrow by evading it today."

— Abraham Lincoln

MENTALLY TOUGH PEOPLE understand that they alone are responsible for their thoughts, emotions and actions, and they refuse to be controlled by external circumstances. They take charge of their lives, own their successes and failures, and never blame others for their problems. They rise to challenges and obstacles, facing them head-on, and proactively take steps to overcome them. You won't find them complaining. They remain calm and level-headed in adversity, responding with calculated and rational actions. They refuse to let outside forces dictate their lives and are fiercely determined to achieve their goals.

They don't shy away from change.

"The only way to make sense out of change is to plunge into it, move with it, and join the dance." — Alan Watts

---

MENTALLY TOUGH INDIVIDUALS embrace change as an integral part of their growth and development. They understand that stagnation and complacency are their worst enemies, and they actively seek new challenges and opportunities to keep pushing themselves forward. They refuse to be bound by their old ways of thinking and are open to new ideas and perspectives. Even in the face of discomfort and uncertainty, mentally tough individuals do not let fear hold them back. They push past their fears, take bold action to achieve their goals and constantly adapt to their surroundings--anticipating and planning for the inevitable changes that will come their way. Their unwavering willingness to embrace change sets them apart from others. They are the masters of their destiny, boldly forging ahead and embracing change with open arms.

They don't expect immediate results.

"Success is not a one-day story; it's a journey that requires commitment, patience, and perseverance." — Tony Robbins

---

MENTALLY TOUGH PEOPLE do not expect immediate results. They understand that success takes time, patience, and perseverance. They set realistic goals and work steadily towards achieving them. They are willing to sacrifice short-term gratification for long-term success.

They view failure as a ladder to success.

"Failure is simply the opportunity to begin again, this time more intelligently."

—Henry Ford

MENTALLY TOUGH PEOPLE view failure as but a stepping stone in their journey. Rather than letting failure discourage them, they use it as fuel to work harder and smarter. They analyze their mistakes and build from lessons learned. Feedback is a requirement for improvement, and failure is the ultimate feedback. Embrace it. If you aren't failing, it means one of two things; either you're not getting out of your comfort zone enough, or you're the best in the world.

They don't let criticism get them down.

"You can't let praise or criticism get to you. It's a weakness to get caught up in either one." —John Wooden.

MENTALLY TOUGH PEOPLE understand that not everyone will support their dreams. They refuse to let the opinions of others define their path in life. They use criticism as fuel to drive them forward, and they surround themselves with positive people who help them stay focused and motivated.

They don't resent other people's success.

"Resenting another person's success is like drinking poison and waiting for the other person to die." — Buddha

---

MENTALLY TOUGH PEOPLE do not let the success of others bring them down. They use it as fuel to ignite their fire and propel themselves forward. They recognize that success is not limited and their turn will come with perseverance and hard work. They see the success of others as proof that it's possible to achieve their own goals, and they use it as motivation to improve their own performance.

WHY DO YOU NEED TO BE MENTALLY TOUGH?

- Mental toughness will help you to perform at your best under pressure and stay focused.
- Athletes face immense pressure to perform at their best. Mental toughness enables athletes to handle this pressure and perform at their peak, especially when the stakes are high.
- Mental toughness allows you to stay calm and composed in high-pressure situations, learn from failures, and push through adversity.

You can turn setbacks into comebacks.

FAILURES, injuries, losses and other setbacks are an expected part of an athlete's career. Mental toughness helps athletes bounce back from these setbacks and continue to pursue their goals.

Dealing with setbacks is a crucial part of being an athlete. Setbacks can come in many forms such as injuries, losses or unexpected challenges. It is common for athletes to experience setbacks at some point in their careers, and how they deal with these setbacks can have a significant impact on their overall performance and success.

Michael Jordan was exceptional in dealing with setbacks. Widely considered as one of the greatest basketball players of all time, Jordan faced numerous setbacks throughout his career, including injuries, losses and personal challenges. Despite these setbacks, Jordan never lost his mental toughness and continued to push himself to be the best. He often used setbacks as motivation to improve his game. After losing in the playoffs early in his career, Jordan spent the offseason working tirelessly to improve his physical conditioning and mental focus. This hard work paid off, as he went on to lead the Chicago Bulls to six league championships.

You can develop self-discipline, perseverance, and focus.

ATHLETES MUST STAY FOCUSED on their goals and maintain their discipline to succeed. Mental toughness helps athletes stay focused, even in the face of distractions or obstacles. Accomplishing your goals will take time. With focus, self-discipline and perseverance, you will achieve your goals.

Staying humble and setting new goals are vital for focus and motivation. New and challenging goals can also prevent boredom. Boredom will kill a training plan faster than failure. So, push your limits and get comfortable being uncomfortable.

You will need mental toughness to improve your physical skills.

MENTAL TOUGHNESS and physical skills work together. Competence breeds confidence, and confidence sets the stage for performance. Let's break this down. Competence is a combination of your knowledge, memory, decision-making, comprehension, and physical and mental skills. You will have to work hard to improve these skills; you will need mental toughness to put in that work. As those skills grow, so will your confidence in them. When you have confidence in those skills, you will execute them in competition. While techniques like visualization and breathwork may provide some benefits, they are insignificant compared to building your skills. The path of competence will lead to confidence and success. Mental toughness will keep you on that path.

It will help you deal with criticism.

MENTAL TOUGHNESS LETS you stay focused on the task at hand and block out the noise. By knowing where you're going and how to get there, you won't be knocked off course by critics. You will instead turn their words into fuel to put in more work.

You have to be good at handling success too.

HANDLING success can be just as challenging as managing failure. Success can bring increased expectations, pressure and distractions, which makes staying focused on your goals very challenging. Mental toughness can help you to maintain a strong sense of self-awareness, focus, and discipline in the face of distractions.

SUMMARY

Many people mistakenly believe mentally tough individuals are born that way. I see this as an excuse for a lack of mental toughness. Avoid falling into this trap. Mental toughness is a skill; like any skill; it can be learned and mastered. Don't confuse a lack of skill with a lack of mental toughness. Some athletes learn faster than others. Often those who struggle the most initially end up going the farthest. Making it to the top will be a struggle, so the sooner you get resilience, the better.

That's enough talk about mental toughness, what it is, and why you need it. Let's get to the "how you get it" part. Where will we start? I'll give you a hint. What would you do first if you were lost in the mountains but had a map? If you guessed "figure out where I am on the map," you guessed right. If you are reading this book, you already have a map, meaning you know what you want to achieve, even if you haven't told anyone else. So let's go figure out where you are on that map.

CHAPTER 2
SELF-ASSESSMENT AND GOAL SETTING: KNOWING YOUR STRENGTHS AND WEAKNESSES

MENTAL TOUGHNESS
AND CONFIDENCE

He sat a little taller in the truck on the drive home. He had gotten a little victory, and that's all he needed.

A STORY

Remember the story from the introduction about my oldest son, Maverick, moving from training with children to training with adults? He went from dominating to being dominated. His confidence faded, and he needed mental toughness to push through.

In the first chapter, we discussed the map and finding our location on that map. Maverick had the map, or at least he knew where he wanted to go. He wanted to beat the people now dominating him on the mats.

I asked him what he thought it would take to do that. He said he needed to get bigger and stronger. "What about your skills? Your techniques?" I asked. He said those were important too. I told him this was an excellent opportunity to build a solid defense. He was smaller and weaker than almost all his opponents, so his techniques would have to be near perfect to be effective.

So, we got to work. We started with his defense, as this is where he would be spending most of his time. It makes little sense to work on moves that you won't get to use when it matters most. This is true for every sport, so master the basics.

One of my Commanding Officers told us that all he expected from us was to be "Brilliant at the Basics." If you look at the best athletes across all sports, you will see athletes who have mastered their skills and are brilliant at the basics. Sure, they can do fancy tricks, but mastering the basics got them to the top. They do the fancy tricks to entertain fans or just because they can.

In addition to working on his defenses, we worked on his finishing mechanics for submissions, specifically the triangle choke. Now we had a plan for developing his technical abilities. What about the other two weaknesses? How would we fix the smaller and weaker part? The smaller part isn't something that can be controlled; he would just have to wait to hit his growth spurt.

The stronger part he could definitely improve and improve he did. He started with body weight type exercises, and after a few months of those, he hit the weights. A friend of mine that is a competitive powerlifter built us a weight-training program and we followed the plan together. He followed the program for 16 weeks and is still going strong years later. During this time, he doubled his bench and deadlift max and tripled his squat max. He began to show visible muscle development, and his technical skills were getting sharp.

I knew it was only a matter of time before he saw a significant breakthrough on the mats during sparring. He had been getting demolished for almost a year, but he kept working and trusting in the plan. After about a year, his day finally came.

He was paired up with a guy in his 20s, brand new to BJJ. Maverick absolutely demolished him. He literally made this grown man cry. This was the turning point. Did it matter that he had beaten this guy? Not really. Should he have beaten him? Sure. What mattered most is that it was a turning point, a realization that all the work had paid off.

This was the moment he started believing in himself. I could see it in his eyes, the "aha!" moment of "Maybe, I can do this. No, I can do this." He sat a little taller in the truck on the drive home. He had gotten a little victory, and that's all he needed. Knowing it was a direct result of the work he had put in made a little triumph even sweeter.

So how about you, do you know yourself? Have you pushed yourself so far out of your comfort zone that your weaknesses are blatantly obvious? How can you improve physically, technically or mentally if you don't know where you are on the map?

SELF ASSESSMENT

False confidence must be broken down to no confidence before it can be built into real confidence.

What is Self-Assessment?

Self-assessment means evaluating your skills, strengths, weaknesses and performance compared to what's required to meet your goals. It's all about becoming the best version of yourself.

Why is Self-assessment Important?

SELF-ASSESSMENT GIVES athletes an honest look at themselves. From this place of honesty and transparency, an athlete can start making real progress mentally, physically and technically. Knowing where you are and where you want to go, you can begin planning how to get there.

Through self-assessment, you will not only gain a deeper understanding of your sport and the skills needed but also self-awareness. The only thing worse than no confidence is false confidence. False confidence must be broken down to no confidence before it can be built into real confidence. False confidence is believing you are good without actually being good. Being good is mastery of the basics. False confidence should not be confused with mental toughness.

"Knowing yourself is the beginning of all wisdom." — *Aristotle.*

When you truly know yourself (self-awareness), you are more coachable. You will see that you aren't perfect and have room for improvement and growth. More importantly, you will be ok with that. It will be easier to deal with criticism and learn from feedback. When you know yourself, you will start learning how to better coach yourself and to allow others who know more than you to teach you.

Advantages of Self-assessment

SELF-ASSESSMENT IS the starting point of becoming elite at anything. Think of it as looking in the mirror and seeing yourself for who you are. It's about knowing your strengths and weaknesses to push yourself to be your best.

When you take the time to do an honest, fact-based self-assessment based on measurable skills, you're getting in the driver's seat of your destiny. You will be able to identify your strengths and weaknesses. Only then will you be able to start improving. Obviously, you need to improve in areas of weakness. What about strengths? Yes, those need to improve as well, but this typically comes later and should not be your first self-assessment. That's right, this is not a one-time thing. This should be done regularly. I recommend self-assessment after reaching each goal. ...More on goals later.

Self-assessment is a skill; the more you do it, the easier it will be. Do it on a schedule or when you reach a new level of your sport. A good schedule looks like this if you play a seasonal sport:

1. Self-assess at the start of the season so you can see where you are and make an improvement plan.
2. Do it again in the middle of the season to see how your training plan is working and what adjustments you should make.
3. Do it again at the end of the season so you know what to work on during the off-season.
4. If you play a year-round sport, devise a logical method of scheduling your self-assessments like the example.

Self-assessment is a powerful tool for growth. Honesty about your abilities and performance boosts transparency in your relationship with coaches, mentors and fellow athletes. Once you acknowledge your strengths and weaknesses, you become coachable. You are ready to listen. You are prepared to improve. You are willing to work. You are ready because you know you need improvement. You no longer view coaches, parents, and mentors as people nagging you. You start seeing them as people trying to help you. You start taking advantage of that help, and **you are grateful for it**.

Increased motivation starts with knowing yourself. By knowing yourself, you can start setting goals and seeing progress toward them. Seeing progress towards a goal is like adding wood to a fire. It keeps your dream alive. Motivation is the fire that fuels you, and you can't let it go out.

Self-assessment leads to discipline. Once you know yourself and genuinely want to improve, you will do what it takes to make that happen. Discipline will become a habit if you want it bad enough. It will also keep you on the path when you're not feeling motivated. In other words, you do it because you need to and not necessarily when you want to.

Self-assessments are not just crucial for athletes. They are essential in school, business, and life. Honest evaluations highlight where you need to learn and grow. If you don't know where you are, how will you see the path to get where you want to be? You won't. So take this step. If you take this seriously, you'll be amazed at its impact.

HOW TO SELF-ASSESS

By now, you should understand the importance of self-assessment and how knowing where you are is crucial for improvement. Remember, you must know where you are to start making meaningful progress toward your goals. So how do you conduct these assessments? You will do it with testing and analysis.

Testing a specific skill should not be a continual thing but a progressive thing. This means that once you have mastered a skill, you do not need to keep testing yourself to see if you have it. Testing and analysis are tools to uncover areas that can be improved, whether they are weaknesses or strengths. As you identify and improve these skills, your confidence will grow. This confidence will turn into trusting those skills, which is where you need to be for optimal performance. **You must move from testing to trust, to perform at the highest levels.** Please make a note of that, because it is quickly forgotten.

Suppose you have done some prior research on optimizing performance. In that case, you have probably read about left brain vs. right brain, flow state, etc. All these ideas have merit, but you really need to know that, if you consciously try to improve a skill, your ability to execute that skill often decreases in the short term. This is the reason why it is hard to improve. We live in a world of instant gratification, and we become easily frustrated with ourselves when we do not see instant results.

Consciously trying to improve a skill means you are thinking about the mechanics while you are doing it. This is part of the testing and improvement phase. When you reach the flow or trusting stage, you won't have to think about the mechanics anymore; you will execute them. Many athletes spend time trying to get their minds in the flow state to optimize performance without first putting in the work to make that possible. I know you will not make that mistake.

Let's look at some assessments or tests you will need to add to your training program, to build physical skills and mental strength.

TYPES OF SELF-ASSESSMENT TESTS

These tests are valuable tools for evaluating your skills, knowledge and overall performance. Take ownership of your development and build a foundation for success by adapting these tests to your situation.

Skill-based Assessments

SKILL-BASED assessments focus on evaluating specific skills relevant to your sport. These tests measure your technical abilities, tactical understanding, physical attributes and other sport-specific competencies. They provide a comprehensive evaluation of your proficiency in executing the fundamental aspects of your sport. Skill-based assessments help identify areas where you excel and areas that require improvement, enabling you to tailor your training and development efforts accordingly.

Physical Fitness Assessments

PHYSICAL FITNESS ASSESSMENTS gauge your fitness level and performance-related factors such as strength, speed, agility, endurance, flexibility and coordination. These tests help you understand your current physical capabilities and identify areas for enhancement. By assessing your physical fitness, you gain insights into your strengths and weaknesses, allowing you to design targeted training programs to improve specific aspects of your athletic performance.

Mental Game Assessments

MENTAL ASSESSMENTS FOCUS on evaluating various mental aspects that impact sports performance. These tests assess mindset, motivation, confidence, focus, resilience, and goal-setting abilities. Mental assessments provide valuable insights into your mental strengths and weaknesses, helping you develop strategies to enhance your mental preparation and overall performance. Understanding your mental game can optimize your mental approach and build resilience in facing challenges.

If your confidence is fading, you want to know why this is happening so you can course-correct it. If you feel like giving up, you need to remember why you wanted to reach your goal in the first place. If you are having trouble focusing, you need to practice focusing.

I used two specific tools to help me with my mental game.

THE FIRST WAS A JOURNAL. I would write down my goals and then make a short daily entry about how I was progressing toward those goals. I quickly noted what I was working on that day, my struggles, and how I felt about it. Whenever I wasn't feeling motivated, I would go back and read my journal. The things I was concerned about and struggling with six months ago were no longer issues. In fact, I had forgotten about them. The journal allowed me to remember how far I had come and put another log on the fire of motivation. Athletes tend to forget success quickly and hold on to failure. A journal lets you hold onto and get motivation from your success. So, I encourage you to start journaling, start by journaling about your self-assessment!

Self-reflection is a powerful tool for unlocking your potential. Self-reflection provides valuable insights into areas that external evaluations may miss. Journaling is a simple and effective way to achieve this. This is something that only you can do.

The second tool I used was a device called a focus band. It is like a little EKG device in a headband. It hooks up to your iPhone, measures your brain waves and can tell when you are focused and not. It sounds like nonsense, but it works well. I wouldn't say you need to use this every day, but it is excellent if you want to learn how to get super focused and be able to replicate it. It helps you to practice focusing. While optional, it's worthwhile if it is within your budget.

Tactical Assessments

TACTICAL ASSESSMENTS EVALUATE your decision-making and strategic thinking skills within the context of your sport. These tests assess your ability to analyze game situations, make effective choices, and adapt to changing circumstances. Tactical assessments enhance your game intelligence and help you better understand strategic approaches to maximize your performance. By identifying areas of improvement in your tactical decision-making, you can refine your game strategy and enhance your performance in competitive situations.

LET'S START ASSESSING

Each type of self-assessment uniquely provides valuable insights into different aspects of your athletic performance. By utilizing these and other tests, you can comprehensively understand your skills, knowledge, physical capabilities, mental strengths and weaknesses, tactical understanding, and personal growth. Armed with this information, you can tailor your training programs, set realistic goals, and focus on areas that will significantly impact your overall performance and growth.

These assessments can be conducted through standardized tests, questionnaires, structured observations, or professional guidance from coaches. The choice of tests depends on your specific needs and goals as an athlete. Discuss these tests with your mentor and coach to find the most suitable one.

Here are 25 questions that you can use to self-assess:

WE DISCUSSED SELF-ASSESSMENT, a powerful tool for gaining insights into your abilities, strengths, and weaknesses. The following 25 questions are meant to give you a starting point for self-assessment. Take some time to think about yourself and your capabilities. Reflect on your experiences and be honest with yourself. Write the questions in your journal and answer them when you know the answer. If your answer changes in the future, update your answer in your journal. These questions are meant to be thought provoking. Feel free to add to this list, or exclude questions that don't apply to you or which you can't answer at the moment. I recommend revisiting the ones you can't answer today and see if you can answer them later. These are also listed out in the workbook with space for you to answer.

1. What was the initial reason behind choosing this sport?
2. What keeps me motivated to continue participating in this sport?
3. If I could accomplish any desired outcome in my sport, what would it be?
4. What physical abilities do I excel at in my sport?
5. What mental strengths do I possess?
6. What is the primary physical obstacle hindering my improvement in this sport?
7. What is the primary challenge preventing me from improving faster in this sport?
8. What factors contribute to a higher risk of injury for me?
9. What level of physical strength is necessary for my sport or position?
10. How can I determine if I have achieved the required level of physical strength?
11. Who can I turn to for assistance when I require help?
12. What skills and qualities do the top athletes in my position possess?
13. What is the most crucial aspect to work on now, to enhance my progress in this sport?
14. How can I maximize the benefits of each training session?
15. How can I contribute to the improvement of my teammates?
16. What steps should I take to ensure I am physically prepared for a game?
17. What factors hinder my ability to perform at my best?
18. How many hours of sleep do I need per night to support my performance?

19. What strategies can I implement to ensure I achieve a restful night's sleep?
20. Which foods provide me with a sense of energy and vitality?
21. How can I effectively prepare myself mentally for a game?
22. What is my preferred method of receiving feedback from my coach?
23. What are the sources of pressure that affect me in my sport?
24. How do I respond and behave when I experience pressure?
25. What indicators suggest that I might be overexerting myself?

Even if you cannot answer all the questions immediately, that's okay. But, reflect upon these questions and try to find their answers whenever possible.

RECORDING AND ANALYZING PERFORMANCE VIDEOS

Recording and analyzing performance videos can be very valuable to you as an athlete. By capturing yourself on video, you can review your actions, movements, and overall performance in a more objective and detailed manner. This process offers many benefits, including the following.

Analyze Technique

VIDEOS PROVIDE a visual record of your technique, allowing you to observe your body mechanics, form, and execution closely. By scrutinizing your movements frame-by-frame, you and your coach can identify any technical flaws or inefficiencies hindering your performance. This analysis enables you to make targeted adjustments and refine your technique for better results.

Timing and Coordination

VIDEOS HELP you assess your timing and coordination in various aspects of your sport, such as hitting a ball, executing a specific move or interacting with teammates. Reviewing these moments lets you identify any timing discrepancies or coordination issues, and work on synchronizing your actions more effectively.

Tactical Evaluation

ANALYZING videos allows you to assess your strategic decisions and game awareness. They allow you to observe your positioning, decision-making, and tactical choices during game situations. This analysis helps you recognize patterns, identify areas where you can make better decisions, and develop a more strategic approach to your sport.

Finding Weaknesses

VIDEOS MAKE it easier to identify weaknesses or mistakes that may have gone unnoticed during a game or practice. You can review specific instances where you faltered or made suboptimal choices. This self-awareness enables you to learn from these errors and avoid repeating them in the future. This is especially helpful for non-team sport athletes.

Progress Monitoring

BY REGULARLY RECORDING YOUR PERFORMANCES, you can track your progress over time. Compare videos from training sessions, games or competitions to see how you have evolved, improved, or addressed previous weaknesses. This visual proof will serve as a motivating factor and provide a permanent record of your improvement.

Once you have gathered feedback and insights, it's time to implement the necessary changes. Work on incorporating the identified improvements into your training routine. Practice the adjustments consistently and monitor your progress over time.

Remember that video analysis is a powerful tool that can contribute significantly to your development as an athlete. By following this systematic approach, you can gain valuable insights, make informed adjustments, and continuously improve your performance. By incorporating video analysis into your training regimen, you can enhance your understanding of the sport, accelerate your skills and make more informed decisions to reach your full potential. You can learn the difference between "feel" and "real" by incorporating video analysis into your self-assessment and training. What I mean by this, is as athletes, we often feel like we are doing something correctly, but the video doesn't lie. The video will allow you to match what you feel when executing a technique to what is really happening. This is a decisive step. Few things are more mentally degrading than feeling like you are doing something right and not getting the results you should. Video analysis mitigates this issue.

FEEDBACK - HOW CRUCIAL IS IT?

"Feedback becomes the breakfast of champions."

— Ken Blanchard

Feedback is a game-changer in your training.

Feedback is precious to you. A coach can observe you in action and identify areas of improvement that you might not notice. Feedback and communication are the secret sauce to coaching. They allow the coach to assess your performance, compare it to your goals and guide you toward reaching new heights. Feedback and coaching go hand in hand, but they're not the same.

From a coach's perspective, I want you to understand the significance feedback has in your development and performance as an athlete and really as a person in general.

Remember, your coach is there to help you. Your coach provides insightful guidance based on their sports knowledge and expertise, which was likely built over a lifetime of being an athlete and then a coach. Their feedback lets you gain valuable insights and advice on improving your skills, techniques and overall performance.

Always take feedback positively. It gives you an objective assessment of your performance. Sometimes, seeing the bigger picture or identifying your weaknesses can be challenging. With their trained eyes, coaches can objectively evaluate your performance and provide feedback based on their observations. This helps you to better understand where you are on your map and where you need to go, to achieve your goal.

Feedback can serve as a powerful motivator and keep you accountable. It lets you know that your efforts are recognized and appreciated. When your coach sets expectations and provides feedback on your progress, it creates a sense of accountability for your performance. This accountability pushes you to work harder and strive for continuous improvement.

You can optimize your performance by using feedback. Your coach can help you fine-tune your skills and techniques, identify areas for adjustment, and suggest alternative approaches to enhance your performance. This ongoing optimization process leads to incremental progress and enables you to reach your full potential.

Accepting and implementing feedback is one of the building blocks of a better and stronger coach-athlete relationship. It establishes clear lines of communication and fosters trust. Knowing that your coach genuinely cares about your development and provides constructive feedback strengthens the mutual connection and creates a positive learning environment.

Feedback highlights your mistakes. Mistakes are a natural part of the learning process. Your coach's feedback helps you understand and grow from your mistakes. It offers guidance on overcoming challenges, making adjustments and extracting valuable lessons from these experiences. This constructive feedback enables you to transform mistakes into opportunities for growth. Mistakes should be expected but not accepted. Don't be afraid to make mistakes, but once the mistake is identified, work to correct the issue so you don't repeat it. We talked about this earlier.

Embrace feedback from your coach as an essential part of your journey. Their guidance, objective assessment, motivation, optimization and support in learning from mistakes are all invaluable to your progress. By recognizing the significance of feedback and actively seeking it, you create a supportive and growth-oriented environment that empowers you to excel and reach new heights.

Let's look into the impact of feedback.

RESEARCHERS HAVE EMPHASIZED the significant impact feedback can have on you. It's been proven that feedback can boost your confidence, motivation and drive to succeed. Your coach is there to motivate, challenge, guide and support you in your journey to greatness, both as an individual and as part of a team.

Not all feedback is created equal; your coach should ensure you get the most out of it. When your coach provides feedback, it's important to remember that it's never personal or intended to bring you down. Instead, it's meant to inspire growth and improvement. The sooner you receive feedback after an event, the better it is for your progress. The exception to this would be if you have a coach with serious anger issues or abusive behavior, but this is rare, and that type of person doesn't last long in any leadership position.

Creating the right coaching environment isn't solely on the coach; it's a team effort.

SURE, coaches play a crucial role in creating an environment that nurtures your growth. They design activities, drills and games that challenge you, involve your teammates and promote a hunger for feedback. As an athlete, it's important to remember that mistakes and failure are not setbacks; they're stepping stones towards success.

When you stumble, it's an opportunity to learn and grow, and when you push your mental and physical limits, you can expect to stumble. With the help of your coach, you can safely push your boundaries and strive for excellence. That's what being coachable is all about!

Why does feedback matter in monitoring your progress?

FEEDBACK IS TRULY a secret ingredient for coaches. It elevates your training and demonstrates their commitment to your development. That's the team effort it takes to build a good learning environment and to build unstoppable athletes. While feedback is a secret ingredient for your coach, it's a secret weapon for you as an athlete. The most successful athletes almost always have outstanding coaches behind them.

So, embrace feedback as an integral part of your journey and unlock your full potential with your coach. Do this and turn setbacks into comebacks.

GOAL-SETTING

Win the battle — win the war.

In the military, the end goal is to win the larger war, whatever that may be. To win the war, there are many smaller missions to accomplish, targets to hit and objectives to meet. We check those boxes on our way to victory. For you as an athlete, the war is achieving your end-goals. You will need to set targets or objectives on the path to achieving your goals. Like commanders, coaches can help you set those objectives. Getting feedback from coaches is like requesting air support on a high-value target; if it's available, use it.

Goals inspire you to push beyond your limits and stay motivated during training and competition. They also provide a measurable way to track progress and assess performance and improvement over time.

Setting performance targets helps you strive for higher levels of achievement and success. Hitting your targets and winning small battles have positive psychological effects. They boost your confidence and self-esteem and inject steady doses of accomplishment and fulfillment on the way to achieving your ultimate goal. Win the battle – win the war.

Goals also force you to be intentional when planning and organizing your training. They help you prioritize time, set deadlines and optimally structure your training, thus maximizing your chances for success.

When you set goals, you form a pact with yourself to stay dedicated, disciplined and consistent in your training and lifestyle choices. Like feedback, goals also create a sense of accountability and commitment. Now I'm really going to blow your mind – if you think about it, isn't achieving your goals the ultimate feedback? I know you're nodding your head because it's a universal truth. Of course it is the ultimate feedback, so let's set some goals.

HOW TO SET YOUR GOALS

Know Where You're Going

First and foremost, you better have found where you are on the map through self-assessment. Now, you must determine your destination by envisioning where you want to be, not only during your athletic career but also when it's over. Whether it's just your family or the whole world, how do you want people to remember you? As a hard worker? As a champion? As an ambassador to the sport? As the greatest of all time (G.O.A.T)? Whether it's winning a championship, representing your country, achieving a personal record, or reaching the highest level in your sport, you must have a clear ultimate goal.

Set Clear, Measurable Objectives

IDENTIFY specific objectives you aim to achieve within a particular timeframe. Make sure these objectives are measurable, to track your progress and success along the way. For example, you may want to increase your bench press by 20 pounds in 3 months or complete a 5K race in under 25 minutes.

Be Realistic and Relevant

WHEN SETTING YOUR GOALS, it's vital to ensure they are realistic. Consider your current abilities, resources, and timeframe, and set challenging yet realistic targets as well. Avoid setting both easy and overly ambitious goals. Easy goals may not provide the necessary motivation, and overly ambitious goals may not be achievable within your desired timeframe.

Relevance is another crucial factor in goal-setting. Align your objectives with your overall athletic development and long-term aspirations. Your objectives should contribute to your growth and performance in a meaningful way.

Establish Urgency

SET time-bound goals to establish a sense of urgency and effectively track your progress. Define specific deadlines or timeframes for achieving each objective. This helps you stay focused and accountable to your goals. For instance, you could aim to increase your vertical jump height by 2 inches within 8 weeks. If improving agility is a priority, you might aim to reduce your 20-meter run time by 0.5 seconds within 2 months.

Create an Action Plan

CREATING an action plan is crucial to turning your goals into actionable steps. Break down each goal into specific tasks, training sessions, and strategies that are required to accomplish them. This will help you stay organized and provide a roadmap for achieving your goals. Regularly track your progress, adjust your plan as needed, and celebrate your achievements.

Review and Assess

IT's essential to review your goals and assess your progress regularly. Be flexible and willing to adjust your goals based on changing circumstances or new insights. Seek support and guidance from coaches, mentors and teammates to stay motivated and focused. Take ownership of your goals by regularly assessing your progress and actively seeking growth opportunities.

SUMMARY

To achieve greatness, you must truly know yourself. You are on a transformative journey of self-discovery to uncover your strengths and weaknesses and unleash your potential. Honest self-assessments are the foundation for growth. Identify strengths and weaknesses, set achievable goals, and measure progress.

Objectively evaluate yourself using performance data, video analysis, coaches, and peer feedback. Use tools like questionnaires and skills tests to uncover areas for improvement. Seek constructive feedback from coaches and peers and set attainable and realistic goals that drive you towards excellence with clear direction and unwavering motivation. By following these steps, you will set yourself up for success and strive towards continuous improvement in your athletic pursuits.

Now that you understand the importance of assessing your skills, getting feedback, and setting goals, you might be asking a couple of questions. How do I break my goals down into actionable steps? What specific things do I need to do to get where I want to go? That's where knowledge comes into play. This is the "you don't know what you don't know" part, so let's dive into that.

CHAPTER 3
SEEKING KNOWLEDGE

MENTAL TOUGHNESS
AND CONFIDENCE

"Knowledge is Power"

—Francis Bacon

Knowledge is a prerequisite of skill. You must gain knowledge if you want to improve your skills. Knowledge is familiarity, awareness, or understanding of someone or something encompassing facts, information, descriptions, or skills acquired through experience or education. One can acquire theoretical or practical knowledge of a subject. As an athlete, the knowledge you seek is how to improve.

You need to learn the things you don't know. It sounds simple, but many athletes make the mistake of thinking they know everything. This type of mindset makes them uncoachable.

FIVE KEY ADVANTAGES

I believe these are the five key advantages of acquiring knowledge:

1. Knowledge is access to new information. When you receive or read new information, factual knowledge facilitates the formation of thoughts. Comprehending oral or written language involves more than just vocabulary and syntax. Even audio or visual knowledge is acquired and retained easily if you know the background knowledge.

2. Knowledge builds your roadmap. It provides confidence and a better understanding of yourself. In my opinion, "self-analysis is the best analysis," which means that anyone who possesses a sense of themselves will know they don't have all the answers. This will change your mindset and give you a willingness to learn. Knowledge aids in making informed decisions in life. The more you learn, the more you realize that learning is a lifelong journey.

3. It simplifies problem-solving. On and off the field, you will face challenges that may initially seem impossible. However, with knowledge, you can enhance your ability to think objectively, whether tackling problems in real-life situations or in training and competition.

4. Knowledge enhances your focus. If you know how to solve a problem, you'll know what to do, you'll be focused, and you'll take action to solve that problem. You eliminate negative thoughts by knowing what you need to do, and you will be able to overcome that little voice of resistance saying, "I can't."

5. Without a doubt, knowledge is a prerequisite to success. With knowledge, significant achievements in life are likely. The more knowledgeable you are in your field, the greater your value will be.

WHY SHOULD KNOWLEDGE BE IMPORTANT TO YOU?

When I coached my son Wyatt's 14U baseball team, I tried to instill the importance of understanding what it takes to win as a team. These things were just fundamentals. Remember when I was talking about being brilliant at the basics? If that is good enough for the SEAL Teams, then it should work for 14U baseball as well.

We had several talented athletes on the team, many of whom were on the championship team the year before. The problem was that the game was fundamentally different jumping from 12U to 14U. They were playing on a bigger field without a run rule. Previous success required good batting and base running, and if they could hit the run limit each inning, they only needed good defense in one or two innings.

Despite my guidance, they remained complacent as a team, unwilling to accept the knowledge I was trying to give them. They relied solely on what had worked in the past, and their initial overconfidence was their downfall. They thought they knew everything. They lost every game. Their overconfidence had to face reality, and their confidence as a team was shattered. A few kids listened and improved considerably, but baseball is a team sport, and you must work as a team to be successful.

Contrast this with my experience coaching my youngest son Ryder's flag football team. This was a group of 9-year-olds that wanted to win. They showed up to practice with great attitudes and a willingness to learn. They weren't all stellar athletes, but they focused on the basics. They learned to hand off, catch, run routes, and they knew the playbook. They learned how to stay in position and defend as a team. They won almost every game. They were a force to be reckoned with. They were able to do this because they were coachable, and they had the knowledge. They understood what it would take to win at their level.

You are in the sport because you love it, or at least you should love it. But you also want to win, right? In your pursuit of excellence, you should actively seek to expand your knowledge base, adapting and evolving to meet the demands of your sport. By acquiring knowledge, you empower yourself to perform at your best and achieve remarkable feats on your path to success. Tell me, are you driven by your desire to win and achieve greatness? One thing that will make a difference is knowledge, so be coachable and go get it.

You must learn your sport's rules, skill sets, strategies and tactics. You should immerse yourself in physical training and conditioning, understanding exercise physiology, biomechanics, and strength and conditioning principles. You must embrace the power of mental preparation and learn techniques to enhance focus, concentration, motivation and resilience.

You must learn to analyze game situations, study your opponents, and acquire tactical and strategic awareness. Stay updated on sports science and technology, utilizing data and performance tracking tools to optimize your training. Prioritize injury prevention, equipping yourself with knowledge of warm-up routines, recovery methods and rehabilitation protocols.

You must absorb the teachings and advice of coaches, mentors and fellow athletes. Be humble – embrace the humility required to admit that you have yet to grasp it all and that there are depths yet unexplored. You should not accept all advice and follow it mindlessly. But you should at least listen to it. Evaluate advice, judge it and see if it feels right. This hunger for knowledge will propel you forward, pushing you tirelessly to seek improvement and break through the barriers that stand in your way.

KNOW YOUR ROLE

"If you are not willing to learn, no one can help you. If you are determined to learn, no one can stop you." — Zig Ziglar

Athletes should focus on developing their skills before joining a team or engaging in sports. Dedicating time and effort to honing fundamental skills, improving technique, and gaining a solid understanding of the sport's principles and strategies should be your focus. If you are already on a team or playing a sport competitively, you need to build your fundamentals in addition to your regular practice sessions.

For example, if you play basketball, you should prioritize polishing your shooting accuracy, ball-dribbling techniques, passing abilities, and defensive moves. You should also work on your physical fitness, agility, and understanding of the game's strategies and tactics. Once you have built a strong foundation of individual skills and knowledge, you are better prepared to contribute effectively to a team environment. You can then seamlessly integrate with your teammates, understand their roles and responsibilities on the court, and perform cohesively as a unit. This analogy applies to every sports team and SEAL Team, where individuals come together to work towards a common goal.

Each athlete is assigned a specific role within the team to maximize effectiveness and achieve success. These roles, both formal and informal, create a cohesive unit that allows the team to reach its full potential. But what happens when there is a lack of role clarity? How does it impact team performance?

Researchers have identified four elements contributing to an athlete's understanding of their role.[1] First, athletes need to know the scope of their responsibilities. Second, they must understand the expected behavior associated with their role. Third, they should know how their performance will be evaluated. Lastly, they need to understand the consequences that arise from failing to fulfill their responsibilities.

Having a clear understanding of your role brings several benefits. It increases your confidence, gives you a sense of purpose and enhances your belief in your abilities. On the other hand, a lack of role clarity can lead to a diminished sense of purpose and lower confidence.

Coaches play a crucial role in improving role clarity within the team. Effective communication is vital. Coaches must clearly articulate their expectations, breaking them into well-defined roles and behaviors. Doing so, they help athletes better understand what is expected of them. This clarity reduces uncertainty, enhancing confidence and motivation to perform.

Athletes who fear failure may be inclined to cover up their mistakes or avoid taking necessary risks. If you are unsure of your responsibilities, it can increase anxiety. It can lead to feelings of butterflies in the stomach and a faster heart rate, which can negatively impact performance. While a certain level of stress can be beneficial, excessive anxiety can hinder performance.

GET THE KNOWLEDGE

As a young athlete, you have access to a wealth of knowledge sources that can help you excel in your chosen sport. You have access to not only your coaches and trainers but also to all the knowledge about your sport. You have the Internet and with it, instant access to knowledge that would otherwise take considerable time to find. Your reading of this book is an example of this. The tricky part is figuring out what is gold and what is garbage. One way to figure this out is to look at the person and make an evaluation based on them. Have they reached elite status in something? Have they built champions? Have they been where you want to go? Suppose the answer to at least one of these questions (or similar ones) isn't yes. You may consider getting information from a different source.

Your coaches and trainers are there to guide and support you. They possess valuable expertise and can provide insights into technique, strategy and physical training. Feel free to seek their advice and take advantage of their experience, to improve your skills and understanding of your role on the team.

Stay curious and do your research. Keep up with the latest findings and advancements in your sport. By staying informed, you can gain a competitive edge and make informed decisions about your training and performance.

You can look up to professional athletes who have succeeded in your sport. Learn from their experiences and stories of both triumph and failure. Their journey can inspire and motivate you to reach new heights. Follow their social media accounts, watch interviews, and read their biographies to gain insights into their mindset, training routines, and the challenges they faced along the way.

Remember, your mental game is just as important as your physical abilities. Your mental skill will need to be built with your physical ones. As your physical skills grow, so will your confidence in them. Your belief in yourself will increase as you achieve small goals and start seeing measurable progress. This will build the mental toughness you need to stay on the path to becoming an elite athlete.

Tap into the knowledge and experiences of your teammates and peers. They are on a similar journey and can offer valuable insights. Engage in discussions, share ideas, and learn from each other's strengths and weaknesses. Together, you can support and motivate one another to improve as athletes.

Explore online resources to supplement your learning. We don't need to reinvent the wheel. When I wanted to become a SEAL, I went to BUD/s, and SEALs trained me. When I left the Navy to play professional golf, I found the best teacher I could. After golf, I went to business school and learned from some of the best entrepreneurs in the world. Before writing this book, I found successful authors and had them coach me. Being willing to learn and actively seeking knowledge has allowed me to go further faster.

STRATEGIES FOR MAXIMIZING LEARNING AND RETAINING KNOWLEDGE

The knowledge and skills you acquire through training are like superpowers; they can propel you toward your goals and give you a competitive edge. Retaining all that valuable information and using it at the right time will keep you ahead of the game. You can adapt to new techniques and strategies and make smart decisions in high-pressure situations. You must set yourself ahead of and apart from the competition. So, actively review and reinforce what you learn, because the more you retain, the stronger and more successful you'll become on your athletic journey.

The Retention Pyramid

THE RETENTION PYRAMID, also known as the learning pyramid or the cone of learning, is a theoretical model developed by the National Training Laboratory. It provides insights into various learning methods and their expected retention percentages.

According to the pyramid, traditional lectures are considered one of the least effective methods for learning and retaining information. On the other hand, reading is more effective as it provides reference material for recalling information. Audio/visual learning content, such as videos, allows learners to absorb information more efficiently.

Learning by demonstration is better when a teacher or mentor shows step-by-step processes and aids in understanding and retaining complex details. Engaging in discussions promotes active and cooperative learning, leading to greater retention.

The learning pyramid indicates that the most effective method is teaching others. I always believe that the teacher learns more than the student. By accurately and correctly teaching a subject to others, individuals not only master the concepts but also enhance their long-term knowledge retention.

TECHNIQUES TO RETAIN INFORMATION

Here are a few techniques that you can employ to retain the information you have learned:

Practice, Practice, Practice

YOU CAN EMPLOY regular practice to reinforce and retain the information you have learned. Consistently engaging in training and practice sessions will help solidify your understanding and memory of the material. By actively participating in the training process, you reinforce the information and improve retention. So, dedicate time and effort to regular practice sessions, to maximize your learning and retention as an athlete.

Learn Actively

INSTEAD OF PASSIVELY OBSERVING OR listening, actively participate in activities that require hands-on involvement and problem-solving. This could include practicing specific drills, engaging in game simulations, or actively analyzing and strategizing during training sessions. You are more likely to retain information by actively participating because it becomes a tangible and experiential learning process. Active learning also helps develop muscle memory, improves decision-making skills, and enhances overall performance.

Use Visual Aids

Use visual aids such as diagrams, charts and visual representations. Visuals can be powerful tools for enhancing memory and understanding. Create or find visual materials that depict the concepts, techniques or strategies you are learning. This could include diagrams illustrating proper form or technique, charts displaying game statistics or tactics, or videos demonstrating specific movements or skills.

Mental Rehearsal

ENGAGE IN VISUALIZATION and mentally rehearse the techniques, strategies and game scenarios you have learned. Close your eyes and vividly imagine yourself executing the skills with precision, making strategic decisions and successfully navigating different game situations. By mentally rehearsing, you reinforce neural connections associated with the learned information and enhance your understanding and memory. This technique can help improve focus, confidence and overall performance.

Break Down into Smaller Chunks

BREAK DOWN complex information into smaller, more manageable chunks. Rather than trying to remember a large amount of data, divide it into smaller, interconnected parts. For example, when learning a new play or sequence of movements, break it down into individual steps or components.

Focus on mastering each chunk before moving on to the next. This approach makes understanding and remembering the information easier since smaller chunks are more digestible for the brain. You build a solid foundation for retaining the entire concept or skill by practicing and reinforcing each chunk separately.

Teach Others

ONE OF THE best techniques to enhance knowledge retention is to teach others what you have learned. When you explain concepts or techniques to others, you reinforce your understanding and memory of the information. Teaching requires you to organize and articulate the knowledge in a way others can understand, deepening your understanding. It prompts you to break down complex ideas into simpler terms, identify critical points, and clarify misunderstandings. Whether you teach a teammate or a friend, it helps solidify your retention and mastery of the concepts or techniques you have learned.

Take Notes

MAKE it a habit to take detailed notes after training sessions, competitions and coaching sessions. Note-taking is an active learning process that helps reinforce and solidify the information in your memory. After these sessions, jot down key points, strategies, techniques and feedback coaches or teammates provide. Be specific and organized in your note-taking to capture essential details. Later, when you review your notes, it will help you recall and reinforce what you have learned.

. . .

Use Technology

UTILIZE MOBILE APPS, video analysis tools, or wearable technology to record and review performance data. These technological tools offer valuable insights into your training and performance, allowing you to track progress, identify patterns, and make informed adjustments. Utilizing mobile apps designed for athletes, you can log and analyze your training sessions, track statistics, set goals, and receive personalized feedback. Video analysis tools enable you to record and review your technique, enabling you to identify areas for improvement. Wearable technology, such as fitness trackers or smartwatches, can provide real-time data on your performance metrics, including heart rate, speed and distance covered.

Be with Positive People

SURROUND YOURSELF WITH POSITIVE, supportive individuals who encourage learning and growth. Engage with coaches, teammates, or mentors who foster a positive and motivating atmosphere. Seek training environments or teams prioritizing knowledge sharing, collaboration and continuous improvement. Interacting with like-minded individuals who are passionate about learning creates an environment where you can exchange ideas, receive constructive feedback, and push each other to excel.

BUILDING A SUPPORT NETWORK

A support system for an athlete is a network of individuals and resources that assist, guide and encourage you in achieving your goals and maintaining your overall well-being. Your support system comprises various people or institutions to help you with your needs. Coaches play a crucial role by providing technical expertise, training programs and strategic guidance to enhance your skills and performance. They motivate you, offer valuable feedback, and help you set and achieve your goals.

Teammates are integral to your support system, offering camaraderie, support and a sense of belonging. They understand the unique challenges of your sport, and their presence boosts morale, encourages friendly competition and fosters a collaborative environment. Sports medicine professionals, such as athletic trainers, physical therapists and sports physicians, work closely with you to prevent injuries, manage existing conditions, and optimize your physical health and well-being.

Your support system should also include strength and conditioning specialists who focus on developing and maintaining your physical fitness. They design personalized training programs, monitor your progress and ensure that you avoid overtraining and burnout. Sports psychologists or mental skills coaches help you manage stress, build mental resilience, enhance focus, develop goal-setting strategies and maintain a positive mindset.

Proper nutrition is essential for your performance, recovery, and overall health. Nutritionists or dietitians work with you to develop personalized meal plans and educate you about fueling your mind and body.

It's important to remember that your support system is unique to you and can vary depending on factors such as your level of competition, available resources and personal preferences. Your support system is vital in helping you thrive as an athlete, providing the necessary guidance and assistance to help you reach your full potential.

Why Do You Need a Support System?

A SUPPORT SYSTEM is crucial for you as an athlete for several reasons. It provides guidance and expertise from experienced coaches, trainers and professionals who can offer valuable insights and help you improve your skills. They can also provide technical advice and strategies to enhance your overall performance.

Coaches, teammates and friends can inspire you to push beyond your limits, encourage you during difficult times and celebrate your achievements. Their presence reminds you to stay committed to your goals and maintain focus.

How to Build a Strong Support System

BUILDING a solid support system as an athlete involves several key steps. Start by identifying your needs and assessing the areas where you could benefit from support.

Once you have identified your needs, seek knowledgeable professionals to provide the specific support you require. Look for coaches, trainers, and sports medicine experts with experience and expertise. Consider their qualifications, reputation, and compatibility with your goals and values.

Find teammates who share your passion for the sport. Surrounding yourself with like-minded individuals who understand the challenges and joys of athletic pursuits can create a supportive and motivating environment. Engage with your teammates, participate in team activities, and build relationships based on mutual respect and camaraderie.

Parents as Support System

I HAVE ALWAYS ENJOYED WATCHING my kids train and compete, and they know that I will be there when they need me. Seeing your parents in the stands during competitions is incredibly motivating. Their presence shows their commitment and belief in your abilities. Their cheers and positive feedback after performances boost your confidence and drive to excel.

Parents can provide vital emotional support by offering encouragement and understanding to you. They can be a source of reassurance to you during both successes and setbacks, listening to your concerns and celebrating achievements.

Parents play a crucial role in your support system. They provide invaluable support and contribute to your overall development and success. Your parents are your emotional anchors, offering unwavering love, encouragement and understanding. They celebrate your victories and console you during defeats. Their belief in you and ability to provide reassurance during challenging times significantly impact your mental well-being. Sometimes parents can be overly supportive by telling you that you are better than you actually are. It's because they love you and want to encourage you, but you should ask your parents to be honest and realistic in their support.

Maintain open lines of communication with your parents. Share your goals, challenges, and progress with them. Discuss any concerns or issues in your sports environment and seek their advice and guidance when needed. Their support and understanding will strengthen your relationship and foster a sense of trust. Take the time to express your gratitude to your parents for their unwavering support. Showing appreciation will deepen the connection and mutual respect within your support system.

Remember, your parents will often be your loudest cheerleaders. By actively engaging with them and nurturing a relationship based on trust and open communication, you can build a strong foundation of support that will uplift and propel you forward in your athletic journey. If you don't have parents that support you, that is unfortunate, but it doesn't mean you can't accomplish your dreams.

SUMMARY

So, to all young athletes, in this ever-evolving world of sports, knowledge is one of the most important prerequisites to building skill. It holds the power to elevate your game and propel you to new heights. Absorb information like a sponge, seek it out relentlessly and embrace it with an insatiable hunger. Immerse yourself in the intricacies of your sport, learn from the greats who have walked the path before you, and dissect every ounce of wisdom they impart. In other words, "nerd out" with your sport.

Knowledge is not a passive pursuit; it demands total commitment and unwavering dedication. So, sharpen your mind, strengthen your body, and seize every opportunity to expand your understanding. Remember, greatness is achieved not only through physical prowess but through the relentless pursuit of knowledge. With the foundation of knowledge, there are no limits to what you can achieve. Now, go forth, armed with the power of knowledge and let it guide you to triumph.

One habit--yes, I say habit—that you must build into your system is deliberate practice. This is so important that I devoted the entire next chapter to it. This is where you will learn how to systematically transform knowledge into skill. So, let's get after it; your new skills await.

---

1. (Inner Drive. (n.d.))

CHAPTER 4
DELIBERATE PRACTICE

MENTAL TOUGHNESS
AND CONFIDENCE

"We are what we repeatedly do. Excellence, then, is not an act but a habit." —
Aristotle

Practice makes perfect. I'm sure you have heard this before. Well, it is not true. Practice makes permanent. Perfect practice makes perfect, meaning you must be intentional with your practice, and quality is more important than quantity. If you practice doing something wrong, you are building motor patterns that you will have to unlearn or override to improve.

I've had several friends ask me to teach them how to shoot, and something that I have found interesting is that complete beginners improve faster than those who have been shooting for many years. The reason for this is that the beginner has no mistakes to unlearn. They have only learned the correct way. Those with experience have to unlearn their bad habits first.

This doesn't mean you should skip practicing to avoid building bad habits. It means that you must become a master of deliberate practice.

Deliberate practice is a focused and systematic approach to improving skills and performance in any field, including sports. This approach is how you will take the knowledge you learn and forge it into skill. I use the word forge for a specific reason. Have you seen something being forged? If you haven't, go online and watch a video of a knife being forged. The process is something like this; the blacksmith heats the metal in a forge until it is glowing and red hot. As the metal is beaten on an anvil, it starts to take shape. This blacksmith repeats the process until the blade has taken form. But it isn't over yet; the blade is then tempered in an oven. Tempering strengthens the blade and prevents it from breaking.

Your first step in building mental toughness is understanding that your journey to becoming elite is no different from that of a knife. You will have to be shaped. This process is challenging and will take many iterations of deliberate practice to shape your mental and physical skills into those of an elite athlete. Once you have those skills, they must be tempered in the oven of competition. Only then can you be elite.

You need to adopt deliberate practice, which distinguishes itself from what is commonly known as "normal" or "regular" practice in sports. Deliberate practice focuses primarily on the seemingly minuscule aspects of your sport, requiring you to set unique and sometimes unconventional milestones. For instance, you might challenge yourself to make 100 free throws or perform a specific maneuver repeatedly. By consistently repeating these actions, you will notice significant improvement over time.

A STORY

After leaving the Navy, I spent three years trying to make it to the PGA Tour. I realized I needed an experienced coach shortly after starting down this path. I needed someone who had taken people to the PGA Tour. I started working with Kevin Kirk. Kevin is one of the top golf coaches in the world and coaches many elite golfers, including major champions.

The first thing we looked at was my training plan. Kevin asked me what a typical practice day looked like for me. I told him I practiced 12-15 hours a day, seven days a week, and listed everything I would do. He listened and then told me a story about a guy who had won some ridiculous amount of Ironman triathlon races. This guy studied the past winners and learned the critical skills required to win these races. He then developed a systematic approach to training these skills. He spent less time training than his competitors, but he trained in the most critical areas that made the most difference in winning.

He explained that this guy had perfected what he would train and figured out how long he could train each day. He did this based on his neurological baseline. That's a big word, and you probably have no idea what that means. It's ok; neither did I.

Your neurological baseline is how much fuel you have in your tank. When you practice, you use fuel mentally and physically. When you eat and rest, you refuel. By practicing 15 hours a day, 7 days a week, I was destroying my neurological baseline and my ability to improve and compete. Let's look at how that works.

Let's say Monday morning, you start with 100 percent. If you overtrain all week, then the following Monday, you will begin with 90 percent. After a few weeks, you start to operate in the 50 percent range. As your baseline drops, you start losing focus, training becomes a grind, your progress slows or reverses, and your risk of injury increases. There are times when you can and should push your limits but keep this concept in mind to know when you need to dial your intensity back.

After telling me this, Kevin asked me what a tournament day looked like. I told him I would typically get to the course about an hour before my tee time (start time), warm up for about half an hour, then play my round. He said perfect; we need to make your training schedule match that. He told me I had five hours a day to get my work in and that I would alternate daily morning and afternoon practice sessions to be accustomed to both. On top of that, he told me I was required to take one day off per week.

Now that we had that covered, he got into the specifics of what each practice would look like. He told me what it took to play at the highest levels and then made a training plan to reflect it. Most readers probably don't play golf, but I want you to apply this principle to your sport.

He told me that winning on the PGA Tour consisted of 4 primary skills:

1. I needed to be able to consistently hit the ball within 15 ft of the pin from 150 yards or closer.
2. Getting the ball within 5 ft of the pin from 20 yards out and closer.
3. Consistent putting from inside 15 ft.
4. Hitting the fairway off the tee.

My training plan needed to both reflect and build these skills. On odd days (meaning the day's date was an odd number), I would hit 3 shots at each odd distance: 35, 45, 55, 65, 75, 85, 95, 105, 115, 125, 135, and 145 yards. On even days, I would hit the even numbers. Next, I would hit three shots with each iron--odd numbers on odd days and even on even days. I would hit one straight, one draw (curves right to left), and one fade (curves left to right). Then I hit three shots with my driver, 3-wood, and my driving iron. I used a full pre-shot routine for every shot as if I was playing a tournament round. This part took one hour. Next, I would work on my short game. I had one hour to practice various shots from around the green. Then I had one hour to practice my putting. I spent 95% of my time practicing from inside 15 ft and the remainder on 30-50-foot putts. After this practice session, I would go on the course and play as many holes as possible in two hours.

I went all in and fully implemented this training program, and it transformed my game. The concept was so simple, I couldn't believe I hadn't thought of it myself. Years later, I realized this concept was the same methodology the Navy used to train SEALs--Not the five hours a day part but the systematic approach to building the skills needed for combat. After business school, I realized this same approach also worked there. Not only does this method work, but I am convinced it is the only method that consistently produces excellence in those who are disciplined enough to use it.

THE 10,000-HOUR RULE

In his bestselling book "Outliers," Malcolm Gladwell outlined the "10,000-hour rule". He suggests that mastering complex skills and subjects, such as playing the violin or reaching the proficiency level of Bill Gates in computer programming, requires approximately 10,000 hours of dedicated and focused practice.

According to Gladwell, the 10,000-hour rule signifies the importance of deliberate, concentrated practice in achieving exceptional expertise. This rule implies that it is not solely innate talent or innate ability that determines success in these areas but rather the significant amount of deliberate practice invested over an extended period.

Gladwell suggests that reaching the threshold of 10,000 hours of practice is an approximate guideline for achieving mastery. He emphasizes that this duration of practice does not guarantee mastery in every field but instead acts as a general benchmark for achieving a high level of proficiency.

Gladwell's popularization of the 10,000-hour rule has sparked discussions and debates within various domains, ranging from sports and music to entrepreneurship and academic pursuits. While some researchers and experts argue that the specific number of hours may vary depending on the field and individual factors, the underlying principle of deliberate practice and dedicated effort remains essential in pursuing mastery.

Ultimately, the 10,000-hour rule serves as a reminder that exceptional achievement in complex skills is often the result of countless hours of focused practice, determination, and perseverance. It highlights the importance of disciplined effort, continuous improvement, and a willingness to invest substantial time and energy to attain expertise in any field.

STRATEGIES FOR EFFECTIVE DELIBERATE PRACTICE

Avoid subscribing to the belief that all practice is equal. Instead, optimize your training time for maximum efficiency, leading to better long-term results. Take an active approach by working diligently to master even seemingly monotonous elements of your sport. This dedication will boost your confidence and deepen your overall understanding and proficiency.

Here are the key elements of deliberate practice for you to consider as an athlete:

Start With Why

If you want something bad enough, you'll be willing to sacrifice and even suffer. If you want something bad enough, you will break through obstacles, even if it takes years. If you want something bad enough, you will overcome failure and turn it into fuel.

DELIBERATE PRACTICE IS HARD WORK. You will need sustained discipline to see results. You will need to know why.

Many believe you can build mental toughness, grit and resilience by doing hard things. And while they may be partially correct, they are settling for good over great. Doing hard things for the sake of doing hard things will have some effect, but this method is a waste of time. If you do something hard, like run a 50-mile ultra-marathon, and your sole purpose is to accomplish something hard, then 90% of the value will be gained the first time.

After the first time, if your sole motivation for doing it was to test yourself, your motivation would fade. Grit focuses on your future goal and enables your mental toughness (grit for future, mental toughness for now). The mindset above lacks the future goal and the why.

Starting with your why is much more powerful. What is your why? Your why is the reason you want to accomplish your goal. You must want it. Doing it because someone else wants it for you doesn't really work, at least not when things get tough.

I made it through BUD/s (SEAL training) because I knew my why. When I was tired, wet, cold, and the most miserable I have ever been before or since, I reminded myself of why I wanted it. I didn't want the suffering or to be tired, wet and cold; I wanted what was on the other side of the suffering, and I knew why.

If you want something bad enough, you'll be willing to sacrifice and even suffer. If you want something bad enough, you will break through obstacles, even if it takes years. If you want something bad enough, you will overcome failure and turn it into fuel.

If you feel your motivation is low, reflect on past performances. Recall a memory of when you overcame a challenge or accomplished something impressive. Read past entries from your journal and remind yourself how far you've come. Athletes who remember such experiences are more motivated to tackle similar challenges.

Make and Implement a Plan

IN THE PREVIOUS CHAPTERS, we went into detail on the importance of self-assessments and gaining knowledge. This is where we will start turning that knowledge into skill. In the SEAL Teams, we learned skills in a crawl-walk-run progression. You need to attack your training in the same way.

Start by learning and understanding the core skills required to win in your sport. If you are in a team sport, you will need to understand not only the sport's core skills but also your position. If you want to make it to the top, you will need to understand the core skills required for every position in your sport. However, you must start with the general core skills and then work toward the positional skills. Core skills are the fundamental skills needed to win in your sport, commonly called fundamentals. Remember, "Be brilliant at the basics."

Now I want you to list all the core skills for your sport in your journal. Then you are going to rank yourself. You will rate yourself red, yellow, or green. Red means you cannot execute this skill in practice. Yellow means you can execute the skill in practice but have trouble executing it in competition. Green means you execute the skill consistently in training and competition.

Any skill marked red or yellow will obviously need to be addressed. Depending on your age, you may not have any red marks, but you should have a bunch of yellow. If you don't have any yellow, it means one of two things; 1) you're the best and need to move up (if there's no higher level, congratulations, you're the best in the world.), or 2) you're not being honest with yourself. In this case, I recommend asking a parent or coach how they would rank your core skills. Ask them to be honest with you, and do not take offense if their answer doesn't align with yours. They want you to succeed, and you will only improve once you honestly assess yourself. Once you understand how badly you need to improve and you know why you want it, you will be ready to put in the work to get there.

Now that you have identified your red and yellow skills, I want you to break them down into a crawl-walk-run progression. I want you to start with the easiest parts of each skill and practice them without moving on until you have mastered them. Once you have mastered the easiest part, move to the next and continue doing this until the skill is green. If you fail a step, go back to the easier version and rebuild, then continue on.

You will also need to continue practicing the skills that you marked green. These skills will need to be maintained and strengthened. Do not neglect them. Your training on these will look a little different, though. I want you to increase the difficulty during your training sessions. You will do this by putting as much pressure on yourself as possible. Do this until you fail, then back it off a bit. Rebuild your confidence with a little less pressure, and then do it again. This can be done in many ways, so get creative. Once you understand that pressure and nerves are all in the mind, you will seek them out because you know what they really mean. They mean you are in the game; you are in the hunt. This is what it's all about, but to get there, you must first get your skills to green and then train yourself to withstand pressure.

Here is a simple example of how I used this principle when coaching my youngest son's football team. The kids were age 7-8, so the core skills were pretty basic-- things like staying in position on defense, not fumbling handoffs, and completing short passes. We worked on developing these skills in a systematic way. Only about half the kids could consistently catch the ball at the first practice. I knew this had to be addressed, so I turned it into a game. As they improved, I made the game a little harder. If they failed, I would make it a little easier. I wanted them to get a little win each practice, but I wanted them to stretch to get it; I tried to put them just over the edge of their comfort zone.

I put ten cones out in a straight line. The closest was about three feet away, and each additional cone was three feet farther than the one before. On the first day, I only used three cones; if you caught the ball, you moved to the next cone. If you missed, you started over. Everyone on the team learned to catch the first practice. They learned because I made the game almost impossible to fail at the first cone. Anyone can catch a ball from three feet away; I mean, it's basically a handoff. As they failed on the farther cones, they would immediately get a little win by catching the ball at the first cone. Their confidence grew quickly, and before long, almost the entire team was completing the drill with ease. So, we had taken their skills from red to yellow and some of them all the way to green.

This was when I started putting pressure on them. For the next couple of practices, I implemented a new rule. You had to run a lap and start over if you dropped a pass. Everyone ran on the first day. After a few practices, they adapted, and almost the entire team completed the drill without running. So, I upped the difficulty again; if someone dropped a pass, the whole team ran. But they each only had to catch one pass, and they could pick any cone, even the three-foot cone. If they could all catch it, not only would they not have to run, but the other coach and I would run. I thought for sure I would be running some laps that day, but there was always at least one kid who insisted on running to the last cone, missing the pass. The entire team ran laps all practice.

At the end of practice, I asked them what they had learned. With some guidance, they concluded that if you know what it takes to win, you should just do that. There is no need to make it harder than it has to be. If you only need a three-foot pass to win, don't go for a Hail Mary. They applied this lesson-learned in the season and had an almost perfect season with only one loss. They ran four simple plays and focused on short passes. Watching a group of kids transform from being unable to catch into athletes executing during competition was truly spectacular.

Use Your Goals and Feedback to Inform Your Training.

THERE IS one thing that you should make sure to do when you are planning deliberate practice that is to set goals. Defining specific, measurable goals is essential to progress toward mastery. Setting goals and breaking them down into small, actionable steps is critical. Converting a general goal, like getting better, into something specific is essential for genuine improvement.

Never shy away from getting some form of feedback for your efforts. This feedback is the key to making deliberate practice genuinely effective. Tracking your progress and receiving feedback makes it easier to fine-tune your practice and stay motivated.

You can track your progress in various ways and finding a system that works best for you is essential. One option is to write down your metrics on a calendar or in your journal, or in the workbook I created to accompany this book. By documenting your performance regularly, you'll have a visual representation of your progress over time. It allows you to see how far you've come and identify areas that need improvement.

HOW VISUALIZATION REALLY WORKS

Your mind holds incredible influence over your actions and outcomes. By repeatedly visualizing success, your brain develops neural pathways that reinforce positivity and build confidence. This will work best with your green and yellow skills. It doesn't work for red skills because you will not really believe something you know isn't true. Visualization is a tool for hyper-focusing and strengthening confidence. You cannot strengthen or focus on something that you do not possess. So, build your skills first. As your skills grow and you start seeing little glimpses of success, remember that feeling. That is what you will visualize. As you get better, you'll have real experience to visualize from and become more confident because you'll know it is true.

FREE BONUS CONTENT DOWNLOAD!

When I was playing professional golf, I met an Olympic swim coach who showed me a form of visualization that could be used to build skills. He used it with Olympians to break world records. I tried it myself, and it works well. I have created a free bonus chapter explaining how you can implement this method. You can download it here. https://mentaltoughnessand confidence.com/visualize-to-actualize/

SCAN ME

ALLOW SUFFICIENT REST AND RECOVERY TIME

Remember to rest in the frenzy of hard practice. Recognize the importance of rest. While intense practice sessions are essential for improvement, you can only expect to maintain that level of intensity for a while. Deliberate practice requires deliberate rest—relax and recharge between sessions.

Just like physical exercise or learning a new language, you can't achieve everything in a single session. Trying to do so often leads to subpar results. Instead, it's essential to incorporate regular breaks into your practice routine. Allow yourself downtime to disconnect from work, engage in activities that bring you joy, and recharge your mind and body.

Balancing periods of focused practice with adequate rest allows your mind and body to recover and rejuvenate. Resting is not a sign of weakness but rather a necessary component of the growth process. It will enable your brain to consolidate learning and prepare for future challenges.

Make rest an integral part of your practice regimen. Listen to your body, take breaks when needed, and engage in activities that bring you relaxation and joy. Incorporating deliberate rest into your routine optimizes your practice sessions and enhances your overall performance as an athlete. Remember, it's all about the Golden Rule of Growth: Stress, Rest, Repeat.

SUMMARY

Deliberate practice is the key to unlocking your true potential as an athlete. It's not about mindlessly going through the motions; it's about pushing yourself beyond your limits, challenging your weaknesses, and relentlessly pursuing improvement.

Embrace the discomfort and the sweat, for you will grow stronger through these moments of struggle. Start with your why, identify core skills, set specific goals, break them into manageable steps, and tackle them with unwavering determination. Remember, it's not just the hours you put in but also the quality of those hours that genuinely matters. So, commit to deliberate practice and watch yourself soar to new heights in your pursuit of greatness.

We are moving along; you have the steps you need to execute. Now let's look at the mindset you need to follow through. You need a mindset that can support you during this phase of growth and skill acquisition. You need the training mindset!

THE MISSING PIECE

"Champions have to have the skill and the will. But the will must be stronger than the skill." — Muhammad Ali

Whether you're a parent, a coach, or an athlete, you probably know all too well that most training programs focus on athletic technique and fitness training over mental resilience.

Yet as soon as a sport becomes competitive – which once it's taken seriously, it inevitably does – that resilience is essential to your success as an athlete.

You're going to face defeat. You're going to face knocks and injuries. You're going to be pushed to your limits. And the secret to dealing with every one of those challenges is having the mental fortitude to pick yourself up, do what it takes to grow, and come back stronger and more focused than ever.

Mental resilience is just as important as athletic ability... yet it's missing from many training programs, and I'm passionate about helping more young athletes to build it. I've seen far too many talented athletes lose faith in themselves and quit before they've had a chance to see what they're really capable of.

I'd like to take this moment to ask you to help me with my mission.

By leaving a review of this book on Amazon, you'll show other parents, coaches, and young athletes where they can find the guidance they need to build the resilience that's so crucial to competitive sports.

SIMPLY BY TELLING new readers how this book has helped you and what they'll find inside, you'll point them in the direction of the part of their training they've been missing.

Thank you for your support. Mental resilience is crucial in the athletic field and life, and I'm determined to help as many young people as I can build it.

CHAPTER 5
THE TRAINING MINDSET

MENTAL TOUGHNESS
AND CONFIDENCE

"I hated every minute of training, but I said, 'Don't quit. Suffer now and live the rest of your life as a champion." — Muhammad Ali

---

M uhammad Ali was not only one of the best heavyweight boxers of all time, but he was also one of the wittiest, most colorful personalities of his era. He won the gold medal at the 1960 Olympics and became the first boxer to win the heavyweight title three times. Just look at his mindset about training when he said. "The fight is won or lost far away from witnesses - behind the lines, in the gym, and out there on the road, long before I dance under those lights."

WHAT IS MINDSET?

Mindset encompasses a person's mental attitude, beliefs and thought patterns that shape their perception and understanding of themselves, others and the world. It influences how individuals interpret experiences, make decisions and navigate their lives.

There are various types of mindsets, including fixed mindset, growth mindset, training mindset and competition mindset.

People with a fixed mindset believe their qualities and abilities are fixed traits that cannot be changed. They tend to see their potential as predetermined and may shy away from things that challenge this belief. Failure is often viewed as a reflection of their limitations, leading to a fear of taking risks.

In contrast, those with a growth mindset believe qualities and abilities can be developed through effort, learning and perseverance. They see challenges as opportunities for growth and embrace failure as a stepping stone toward improvement. They have a hunger for knowledge, are willing to take risks, and they understand that hard work and dedication can lead to personal development and success.

Mindsets are not fixed traits and can be developed and transformed over time. Individuals can cultivate a growth mindset with self-awareness, intentional effort and a willingness to challenge and reframe beliefs. This mindset, characterized by resilience, a passion for learning and confidence in one's capacity for improvement, is often associated with tremendous success, personal fulfillment and overall well-being.

Understanding and harnessing the power of mindset can profoundly impact various aspects of life, including relationships, career, education and personal growth. Adopting a positive and growth-oriented mindset can unlock your potential, help you embrace challenges and cultivate a sense of empowerment and fulfillment.

———

Most athletes overestimate the progress they can make in a month and underestimate the progress they can make in a year or two.

TRAINING MINDSET

ADOPTING a training mindset means focusing on skill development rather than just outcomes. This empowering approach encourages individuals to prioritize the process and invest in building their mental and physical abilities.

With a training mindset, individuals can identify their strengths and weaknesses and work towards consistent improvement. This leads to a sense of momentum and progress rather than frustration from not reaching a particular goal.

A training mindset for an athlete is a mental approach that prioritizes growth, improvement and continuous learning. It involves a deliberate focus on the training process, setting specific goals, and maintaining a positive and proactive attitude toward development.

With a training mindset, you shift your attention away from proving yourself to others. Instead, your primary focus is on personal growth and maximizing your potential. You should know that progress comes from consistent effort, dedication and a willingness to push beyond your comfort zones.

One key aspect of a training mindset is taking a long-term perspective while setting short-term goals. Athletes must recognize that improvement is gradual and that steady progress over time leads to significant advancements. They set goals as discussed earlier in this book, to guide their training and track their progress.

Within a training mindset, athletes become highly attentive to the details of their performance. They analyze their techniques, physical conditioning and mental approach, looking for areas of improvement. They actively seek feedback to identify weaknesses and make targeted adjustments.

Athletes with a training mindset approach challenges as opportunities for growth rather than obstacles. They embrace adversity, setbacks and failures as valuable learning experiences. They view each hurdle as a chance to gain resilience, learn from mistakes and refine their skills.

Developing a training mindset requires discipline, self-motivation and a strong work ethic. You must be willing to put in consistent effort, even when motivation is lacking. Ensure that you understand that actual growth occurs through disciplined practice, repetition and a commitment to the improvement process.

Coaches play a crucial role in fostering a training mindset among athletes. They provide guidance, support and structure, to facilitate growth and improvement. Coaches will help you set realistic goals, create training plans and offer constructive feedback to fine-tune your skills.

Understand that progress is a long-term process; you must focus on consistent effort and deliberate practice. With this mindset, you can unlock your full potential, enhance your performance and achieve your goals.

Impact of Not Having a Strong Training Mindset

NOT HAVING a strong training mindset can negatively impact you in several ways. Without a strong training mindset, you will be hesitant to push out of your comfort zone. You will be afraid of failure and will become risk-averse. You will stick to the things you are best at and neglect to develop the skills you need. Even if you push outside your comfort zone, without a training mindset, you will be easily frustrated and lose motivation in the face of obstacles and failure.

Without a training mindset, you will struggle with resilience and perseverance. When faced with challenges and setbacks during training or competition, you may quickly become discouraged and give up. This can hinder your ability to bounce back from failures and learn from your mistakes, ultimately limiting your progress.

Not having a strong training mindset can hinder your ability to set and achieve goals. Goal setting is a crucial aspect of your athletic development. Without the mindset to set ambitious and attainable goals, you may struggle to track your progress and measure your success. This lack of direction can impede your overall growth and limit your long-term potential.

Developing a Training Mindset

MOST ATHLETES OVERESTIMATE the progress they can make in a month and underestimate the progress they can make in a year or two. Developing a training mindset is deciding that you are focused on skill acquisition, which is the most important thing for you right now. You are not concerned with winning in practice. We all want to win, but sometimes focusing solely on winning at your current level will prevent you from building the skills you need to compete at the next level.

Imagine two 10-year-old competitive swimmers. Swimmer 1 is much taller and stronger than the other kids and is solely focused on winning; he relies on physical attributes alone and doesn't think he needs to get better since he consistently wins. Swimmer 2 is average size and average speed but wants to get better. He realizes that he will need to improve his technique to get faster. He listens to the coaches at each practice and swim meet, and he keeps trying to improve. He tries to beat his best time and studies his training videos to review and refine his technique.

Which swimmer would win after two weeks of this? Swimmer number 1would most certainly win. How about after five years? It wouldn't even be close; swimmer 2 would dominate. All athletes need this training mind-set. Even those at the top utilize a training mindset.

A Training Mindset is a Growth Mindset

A GROWTH MINDSET will increase your motivation, confidence and productivity. A growth mindset will unlock your potential. Fear of failure becomes a thing of the past. You'll be eager to take calculated risks that can propel you toward success. Learning new skills and self-improvement will become second nature to you.

Shift your mindset to focus on progress instead of perfection. Don't let the idea of being flawless control you. Remember that mistakes lead to growth and development. Embrace the journey towards improvement by taking small steps forward.

Welcome constructive criticism as an opportunity to grow and improve. By being receptive to feedback, you can gain valuable insights and knowledge from others. Use their critiques to make necessary changes and enhance your skills. Remember, criticism is an essential tool on the path to personal and professional success.

Acknowledge Your Progress

Recognize and celebrate your small victories, no matter how minor they may seem. Even the smallest improvements can help to keep you motivated.

Own Your Mistakes and Failures

THEY ARE valuable opportunities for growth and development. Don't point fingers or make excuses. Take responsibility and use it as a chance to improve.

Surround Yourself with Positive People

SURROUND yourself with a network of supportive family and friends who challenge, encourage and propel you toward achieving your goals. With a solid support system, you'll stay motivated and focused on your path to success.

WHY IS STRONG MOTIVATION NECESSARY?

When you're motivated, putting in the work is much easier and doesn't feel like work. No one has to make you do the work; you do it willingly. When you're motivated, you're coachable.

Motivation is the driving force that propels you toward your goals and aspirations. It is the fire within you that fuels your determination to succeed and pushes you to give your best effort in training and competition.

Motivation is influenced by several factors. It's essential to understand your why, meaning why you want to achieve your goal. The stronger your why, the more likely you will stay motivated and committed to the journey ahead. Take time to reflect on why you want to achieve your goal and connect with the passion and enthusiasm that lies within you.

Conditioning, mental preparedness and training will ensure that you become better athletes. With motivation, you will be disciplined to put forth your best effort daily.

Conversely, you need to know what you will miss out on if you don't accomplish your goals. When I went through SEAL training, I knew that I would end up on a ship somewhere if I failed. There is nothing wrong with being on a ship, but for me, being a SEAL was the only acceptable outcome.

On days when my motivation was low, I remembered how bad I didn't want to be on a ship. I've found that sometimes you have to focus on what the negative outcome will look like, to jumpstart your motivation and get you back on track.

Some of you may be working towards becoming a professional athlete. If you fail, you will have to get a regular job. There is nothing wrong with getting a regular job, but if you need a jumpstart to your motivation, you may need to reflect on how bad you don't want a regular job.

Your expectations play a crucial role in motivation as well. Set high but realistic expectations for yourself, knowing that you have the ability and potential to achieve great things. Embrace the challenge of pushing beyond your limits and constantly striving for improvement. Believe in your capabilities and let that belief motivate you to reach new heights.

You will undoubtedly face obstacles, setbacks and challenges as an athlete. Motivation helps you solve problems by encouraging you to seek creative solutions and persevere when things get tough. It gives you the mental strength to push through adversity, overcome barriers and stay focused on your long-term objectives and goals.

Motivation also enables you to change old habits that may hold you back. It empowers you to step out of your comfort zone and embrace new training techniques, strategies and approaches that will lead to growth and improvement. It allows you to break free from limiting beliefs or self-doubt, encouraging you to push boundaries and reach for excellence. Remember, motivation is not just about the result; it's about embracing the journey and enjoying the process. Embrace the challenges and opportunities that come your way, for they provide valuable learning experiences and opportunities for growth.

I encourage you to tap into your inner motivation. Discover what truly drives you and connects with your passion for the sport. Set meaningful goals, visualize success and stay committed to your training. Embrace challenges, stay focused and maintain a positive mindset. With unwavering motivation, you have the power to achieve greatness and fulfill your potential as an athlete.

Strategies for Staying Motivated

STAYING motivated is essential for your continued growth and success. Here are some tips to help you maintain your motivation and overcome any setbacks that may come your way.

Take the time to assess your goals and track your progress. It's essential to see how far you've come, as it can be a powerful motivator and self-esteem booster. Remember to celebrate your achievements, regardless of how small they may seem, as they all contribute to your overall progress.

Keep the fire of motivation alive by constantly setting new goals. Think about what you want to achieve in the short term, such as the next week or month, and in the long term, like the next year or beyond. Focusing on one goal at a time will prevent you from feeling overwhelmed and allow you to direct your energy more effectively.

Building new habits takes time and consistency. Stay committed to your routine and keep up the momentum. It usually takes around two months to develop a new habit, but it may take longer for some. Everyone is different, as are their training regimens and mindsets. Sticking to your routine and making it a part of your daily life will eventually make the new habit more automatic and easier to maintain.

Seek guidance from experienced mentors in the areas you want to improve. Look for groups who share your interests and have similar goals and connect with them. Surrounding yourself with positive people who believe in your potential will motivate and support you during challenging times.

What if you lose motivation?

If you lose motivation along the way, don't worry. Setbacks are a normal part of any journey. Take a step back and evaluate whether your goals are realistic within the given timeframe. It might be necessary to break them down into smaller, more achievable milestones. Adjusting your goals can provide a fresh perspective and reignite your motivation.

Seek inspiration from others and surround yourself with inspiring stories and individuals who've achieved similar goals. Read books, listen to podcasts or have conversations with mentors, friends or family members who've successfully seen their aspirations fulfilled. Their experiences and advice can reignite your motivation and provide valuable insights.

Sometimes, all you need is a break to recharge and reset. Allow yourself time to relax and rejuvenate, and return to your goals with renewed energy and enthusiasm.

Remember, it's natural to experience fluctuations in motivation. If you struggle, contact someone you trust, such as a mentor, coach or counselor, who can provide helpful strategies and support to help you navigate challenging times.

Stay committed, stay focused, and always keep in mind the potential that lies within you. You can achieve greatness and reach your goals. Keep pushing forward and embrace the power of motivation on your journey to success.

HOW TO DEAL WITH STRESS AND OVERCOMING BARRIERS

To deal with stress in sports, you must know how to manage it effectively. You can try various techniques during practice to determine what works best during competitions. Start by practicing deep breathing. Hold a deep breath for about five seconds, then slowly release it. Repeat this exercise five times to help calm your mind and body.

Another helpful technique is engaging in muscle relaxation. You can do this by tightening a group of muscles for approximately five seconds and then releasing them. Start with your toes, then to your calf muscles, quads, hams and so-on, to release tension and promote relaxation.

Visualization can also be beneficial. Try imagining a peaceful place or recalling a joyful event. See and feel the stress flowing away from your body. You can also try visualizing yourself completing a pass, making a shot or scoring a goal. This technique can boost your confidence and help you perform at your best.

When you're on the field, focusing on the present moment is essential. Stay fully aware of your surroundings and sensations and avoid getting caught up in worries about the future or dwelling on past mistakes. By staying focused and centered in the present, you'll be better equipped to handle stress.

A consistent routine can help you stay organized and control your stress levels. Having a structured approach to your training and competition can reduce anxiety and provide a sense of stability.

Challenging negative thoughts is another powerful strategy. Replace those negative thoughts with positive affirmations. Remind yourself that you learn from your mistakes, are in control of your feelings, and can achieve your goals. Embrace a positive mindset to counteract stress and boost your confidence.

By incorporating these techniques into your routine, you'll be better prepared to deal with stress and overcome any barriers that come your way. Finding the most effective stress management techniques may require some experimentation. Explore these strategies during practice and incorporate the ones that work best for you into your competition routine.

SUMMARY

This chapter explored the importance of the training mindset for young athletes. A strong training mindset is crucial for growth and success, and allows you to be focused on skill acquisition above all else, even if it means losing sometimes.

By having a training mindset, you are able to turn knowledge into skill. You'll break down your goals into smaller, achievable steps and build momentum and motivation with each little win. Remember, you just need to get one percent better each day. Your motivation will keep you going; if you lose it, make your goals a little easier and remember your why.

If you adopt this mindset, you will see results. Your skills will increase, and even though you aren't focused on winning, you will start winning more.

What does all this have to do with mental toughness in sports? Well, it's the foundation for resilience, mental toughness and grit. You start with your why and then get the knowledge and mindset that gives you the greatest chance for success. This powerful combination stacks the odds in your favor, allowing you to start stacking small wins and increase your motivation. As your motivation grows, you will work even harder and get even more wins. If it falls apart and you lose motivation, reboot the system, reset your goals and start again.

Once you've built your skills and are ready to take your execution to the next level, you must master the competition mindset. Always be conscious of what mindset you are using, as it will dictate how you act. With the training mindset, the focus is on skill acquisition. With the competition mindset, the focus is on winning. A training mindset takes risks and pushes outside of the comfort zone so you can grow. A competitive mindset is calm and calculating; you play the percentages and stick with what you do best. You only take calculated risks when it's absolutely necessary in order to win. Are you ready to learn how to win?

CHAPTER 6
MASTERING THE COMPETITION/HIGH-PERFORMANCE MINDSET

MENTAL TOUGHNESS
AND CONFIDENCE

"Winning isn't everything, but wanting to win is."

— *Vince Lombardi*

Imagine this scene: The stadium is alive with electric energy, the crowd roaring in unison. Every eye in the house is fixed on that one athlete, the hero of the hour, carrying the weight of a million expectations. The deafening roar of the crowd turns into doubt and anxiety. The air crackles with excitement, and there's a sense that something extraordinary is about to happen. But then, in that split second, it all goes awry. The athlete falters, loses their rhythm, and the expectation of a great victory turns into an embarrassing defeat.

Have you ever wondered why these incredible champion athletes, the ones we cheer for and idolize, sometimes crumble under pressure and choke at the most critical moments? It's a rollercoaster of emotions, filled with drama, anticipation and heartbreak, that leaves us all on the edge of our seats. So, let's dig deeper into what happens when the pressure becomes too much to handle.

First, why does this happen? Why do these seemingly invincible athletes succumb to the pressures of the moment, leaving us bewildered and heart-broken? Well, my friend, it's time to step into their shoes and explore the depths of the human psyche, where fears, doubts and insecurities intertwine.

Remember that choking in sports doesn't make them weak; it tells us they're humans. It's a reminder of the immense pressure they bear and the courage it takes to step onto that stage knowing that failure is a possibility. So, let's appreciate the courage it takes to pursue their dreams, even when the chips are down.

Choking in sports is where highly skilled and experienced athletes under-perform or make critical mistakes during important moments or high-pressure situations. There are various reasons why this may happen, and I'll provide a few examples from actual events to show this choking phenomenon.

The Los Angeles Clippers were considered one of the favorites to win the NBA championship in 2020. However, they blew a 3-1 lead in the Western Conference semifinals against the Denver Nuggets. The Clippers failed to close out the series, lost three consecutive games and were eliminated from the playoffs. Their inability to perform at a high level in crucial games was widely criticized as choking.

Greg Norman, an Australian golfer, had a six-shot lead going into the final round of the 1996 Masters tournament. However, he shot a final round of 78 and lost the tournament to Nick Faldo. Norman's performance was widely regarded as a classic case of choking under pressure, as he failed to maintain his composure and make the right shots during the final round.

Jana Novotna, a Czech tennis player, was leading in the final against Steffi Graf at the 1993 Wimbledon Championships. However, she faltered under pressure, making several errors, eventually losing the match. Novotna famously broke down in tears and was consoled by the Duchess of Kent, highlighting the emotional impact of choking in sports.

These examples demonstrate that even the most talented athletes can succumb to pressure and experience moments of choking. The intense scrutiny, high stakes and psychological factors can all contribute to athletes' inability to perform at their best during critical moments in sports. It reinforces the notion that even the best athletes can experience significant performance declines in critical moments, leading to adverse outcomes.

WHAT IS A COMPETITION MINDSET?

A competition mindset is a mindset for increasing concentration that enables an athlete to effectively focus on the moment and excel in high-pressure situations. It is a mindset that unlocks your potential. It is the mindset that helps you find the zone, flow state, optimal performance, etc. It will only work if you have spent time developing your skills, so build them first.

With a training mindset, your focus is on growth and skill acquisition. With the competition mindset, your focus is on winning. With the training mindset, you will constantly push outside your comfort zone and try new things. You do this to develop your skills and get comfortable in a competitive environment. Have you ever been nervous about doing something, but after you did it a few times, the nerves went away? I'm sure you have; the training mindset helps you reach this point.

The competition mindset is about playing the percentages, using the skills you know you can execute, and using techniques to execute at the highest level possible. This is not the time to try new things. This is not the time to take unnecessary risks. If all it takes to win a football game in the final seconds is to take a knee, then take a knee. Don't go for an 80-yard Hail Mary and give the other team a chance to win.

The competition mindset is strategic. You will study your opponents or, in sports like golf, you will study the course. You will determine a strategy based on your skills of how you will win. You will determine contingency plans for when your strategy fails. The more you can plan and systematize ahead of time, the better you will be. Sometimes in the heat of competition, it can be hard to make the best decision; by having a system, you will make better decisions, and your odds of winning will increase.

When I first started playing professional golf, I lacked this plan. My plan for each tee shot was obviously to hit the ball in the fairway. Much like a pitcher's plan is to throw strikes. But what happens when you don't hit the fairway or you throw the ball past the catcher? You need a plan, and it needs to be second nature.

Initially, if I were to hit a ball in the woods, I would try and hit some miracle shot. I would try to hit it under one tree, over another, and curve it towards the hole. When it worked, it was awesome. The problem is it only worked about 10 percent of the time. When it worked, I would make par or birdie; when it didn't, I would make a double bogey or worse. These big numbers would kill my round. I would make one bad shot, and then a lousy decision would compound the error. If you go down this path for a while, your confidence will undoubtedly take a hit.

A friend named Brian Bailey, a college golf coach, asked me if I had ever looked at golf statistics. I told him that I had not. He sent me a few articles, and I studied them. After reviewing them, we discussed my decision-making process. I learned that if I hit the ball in the woods, all I needed to do was get the ball back in the fairway at around 100 yds from the hole. From 100 yds out, the average professional took 2.5 shots to get the ball in the hole. If I could get the ball back in play, the worst I would make would be a bogey. You can recover from a bogey. I quit trying to hit shots with a 10 percent success rate and went after ones with a 90 percent success rate. I stopped compounding errors by making good decisions. I did this by having a system.

IF GOLF IS YOUR SPORT, use this example in your system. If golf is not your sport, you can still use and apply this concept to your sport. Remember, the key is playing the percentages. If you make good choices, you'll have more chances to win throughout your career. If you have the skills and systematically employ them, you will perform at levels you only dreamed of. Why is this? It comes back to confidence.

If you're using your skills and playing the percentages, meaning you are picking the plays where you have a 70-90 percent chance of success, then you are setting yourself up to get a bunch of little wins. These little wins build your confidence. That is self-belief.

First, you must build your skills using the training mindset. Once you have the necessary skills, use the competition mindset and play to win. The competition mindset is about getting in the zone and taking emotion out of decision-making. The competition mindset takes calculated risks only when necessary to win. Whether you win by 1 point or 100 points, winning is winning.

HOW TO DEVELOP HIGH-PERFORMANCE MINDSET

It's often said that high-performance leaders with a high-performance mindset have no limit on their growth and success.

A high-performance mindset in sports means a mental state and approach that enables athletes to consistently perform at their best and achieve optimal results. It involves a combination of many factors and intense preparation. Athletes with a high-performance mindset can overcome challenges, maintain composure under pressure and consistently deliver exceptional performances.

Motivation is an essential aspect of a high-performance mindset. Michael Phelps, the most decorated Olympian of all time, maintained unwavering motivation throughout his career, constantly setting new goals and pushing himself to break records.

Athletes with a high-performance mindset can concentrate on the task, blocking out distractions and maintaining a laser-like focus. They remain fully present in the moment, enabling them to make split-second decisions and execute their skills with precision. Serena Williams, one of the greatest tennis players, is known for her exceptional focus and mental toughness on the court, allowing her to consistently perform at a high level, even in high-pressure situations.

Confidence plays a significant role in a high-performance mindset. Those who maintain a positive self-image embrace challenges as opportunities for growth. Usain Bolt, the world's fastest sprinter, exuded confidence in his performances, displaying his signature lightning bolt pose before and after races, demonstrating his unwavering belief in his abilities.

Resilience is an essential characteristic of athletes with a high-performance mindset. They can bounce back from setbacks, learn from failures, and maintain a positive attitude. They view obstacles as temporary setbacks rather than permanent roadblocks. The legendary NFL quarterback Tom Brady has displayed remarkable resilience throughout his career, bouncing back from injuries and setbacks to win multiple Super Bowl championships.

Mental preparation is an essential aspect of a high-performance mindset. Athletes who engage in mental strategies such as visualization, goal-setting, and positive thinking are better equipped to handle the pressures of competition. They mentally rehearse their performances, envision success and develop strategies to overcome potential challenges. Gymnast Simone Biles, widely regarded as one of the greatest gymnasts of all time, incorporates extensive mental preparation techniques into her training routine, which helps her perform complex routines with exceptional precision and grace.

You can train yourself to lead with a mindset built for resilience, daring, and innovation to achieve new levels of success.

HERE ARE **three ways you can develop a high-performance mindset:**

1. Master the Path to Excellence Through Discipline

DEVELOPING SUCH a mindset requires discipline and striving for excellence in your training. Discipline is a crucial element of this mindset. By consistently engaging in rigorous and disciplined training over time, you can cultivate the qualities of intelligence, grace and confidence. This process molds the mindset into one that is resilient and capable of performing under intense pressure.

You can achieve excellent results once you commit yourself to a structured training regimen and consistently adhere to it. You must prioritize your training, make sacrifices and dedicate time and effort to continuously improve. By embracing discipline, you will develop the mental fortitude required to overcome obstacles and maintain focus, even in the face of adversity.

You should recognize the importance of mastering the fundamentals of your sport. Understand that excellence is built upon a strong foundation of basic skills and techniques. You will continually refine and strengthen your core abilities through disciplined training, ensuring you have acquired a solid base to build more advanced skills.

As you dedicate yourself to disciplined training and strive for excellence, you will develop a deep sense of intelligence, grace and confidence. You will become highly attuned to your sport, acquiring a profound understanding of its nuances and intricacies. This intelligence will allow you to make split-second decisions and adapt quickly to changing situations during competition.

Grace emerges from the seamless integration of physical abilities, technical skills and mental composure. Athletes with a high-performance mindset exhibit fluidity and elegance in their movements, executing their techniques with precision and finesse. This grace is a testament to their relentless pursuit of perfection through disciplined training.

Confidence is a natural byproduct of disciplined training and the pursuit of excellence. You should consistently challenge yourself and strive for mastery to develop a deep-rooted belief in your abilities. This solid confidence will enable you to perform at your best, even in high-pressure situations, because you have the trust in your preparation and ability to deliver when it matters most.

A high-performance mindset is forged through disciplined and rigorous training, focusing on achieving excellence. You can develop intelligence, grace and confidence by actively seeking out challenging tasks, embracing discipline and mastering the fundamentals. This mental toughness will equip you to perform under extreme pressure, allowing you to excel in your chosen sport.

2. Unleash the Power of Concentration

MAINTAINING focus is one of the reasons why peak performers are successful. Practice focus by aiming your attention at the right things at the right time and staying on course without emotion, bias and distraction.

By developing the ability to direct attention to the right things at the right time without being swayed by emotion, bias or distraction, you can cultivate a mindset that will let you consistently perform at your best.

A high-performance mindset requires a clear vision—a touchstone that guides your actions and decisions. This vision is a constant reference point you can turn to when confused or uncertain. By having a well-defined purpose and direction, you can better channel your focus and avoid getting sidetracked.

To maintain laser-like focus, you must practice directing attention to the appropriate areas during training and competition. Learn to filter out distractions and concentrate solely on the task at hand. This involves consciously prioritizing your attention and avoiding distractions.

Emotional control is a critical element of maintaining focus. You should understand the importance of managing emotions and not allowing them to disrupt concentration. I will not tell you that you need to turn off your emotions because I don't think it's possible, especially when it is something you really want to achieve. So, instead of trying to shut off your feelings, learn to channel them into increased focus.

Distractions are inevitable but learn to minimize their impact. Develop strategies to effectively manage distractions, such as creating a routine, using visualization techniques, or employing mental cues to bring your focus back to the present moment. Understand that maintaining focus is a skill that can be honed through practice and discipline. Tiger Woods's father, Earl Woods, used to try and distract Tiger before every shot. He would yell in his backswing or jingle the change in his pocket when trying to make a putt. Eventually, Tiger learned to tune it out. If you need help with distractions, take the approach that Tiger did. Have someone try and distract you when you practice so you can develop the skill to tune out the noise. Developing this skill will allow you to stay present in the moment.

3. Think Differently to Make an Impact

DARING TO THINK DIFFERENTLY IS a critical component of a high-performance mindset. Winners succeed by challenging conventional thinking and using innovative approaches to solving complex problems. By thinking laterally and creatively, you can break free from constraints and discover unique solutions, allowing you to consistently excel in your chosen sport.

High-performing athletes understand the importance of thinking well, both logically and creatively. Logical thinking allows you to analyze situations, identify patterns, and make rational decisions based on evidence and data. Utilize critical thinking skills to assess challenges and develop effective strategies to overcome them.

STRATEGIES FOR PREPARING FOR COMPETITION

Preparing for competition is essential for maximizing your performance and increasing your chances for success. Adequate preparation allows you to enhance your skills, build confidence, and develop a focused mindset. Here are five steps to adequate preparation:

1. Develop Your Training Plan

DEVELOPING a training plan requires focusing on skill development and technique while incorporating strength and conditioning exercises. You should carefully design a program that targets the specific areas you need to improve in order to excel in your competition. Stay disciplined and committed to the training process, consistently following your plan and pushing yourself to achieve your goals.

2. Prepare Mentally

IMPLEMENTING mental preparation techniques is essential for success in competition. Use positive thinking to boost your confidence and maintain a strong mindset. Embrace the stress of competition and channel it into positive energy that fuels your performance. Recognize that stress can be a motivating force, and use it to your advantage. Everyone gets nervous and being nervous means you care about the outcome. Sometimes, just this realization is enough to calm your nerves.

3. Practice Visualization

PRACTICE VISUALIZATION TO enhance your performance. Imagine executing flawless techniques, achieving your goals and surpassing your opponents. Visualize the entire competition experience, including the challenges you may face, and see yourself overcoming them with confidence and skill. This mental rehearsal will help you feel more prepared and increase your chances of success.

4. Set Clear Goals

DEFINE what you want to achieve and establish measurable objectives. Study and analyze your opponents to gain insights into their strengths and weaknesses. This knowledge will enable you to develop strategies and tactics that give you a competitive edge. Understanding your opponents will also help you adjust your training and preparation accordingly.

. . .

5. Have a Nutrition Plan

CREATE a nutrition and hydration plan to optimize your physical performance. Properly fueling your body with nutritious foods and staying hydrated is vital for peak performance. Consult with a nutritionist or sports specialist to develop a plan that meets your needs.

Proper rest is tied to nutrition as well. Maintain a consistent sleep schedule to ensure you are well-rested and ready to perform at your best during competition. A good night's sleep plays a significant role in your overall physical and mental well-being.

MANAGING STRESS AND NERVES DURING COMPETITION

"Everything can be taken from a man but one thing: the last of the human freedoms — to choose one's attitude in any given set of circumstances, to choose one's own way."

-Viktor E. Frankl - Man's Search for Meaning

PICTURE THIS...

You're standing at the starting line of the sprint finals, waiting for the starting gun to fire. Your heart races, pounding in your chest with an anxious beat. Sweaty palms betray your nerves as if trying to escape the tension. A swarm of butterflies flutters restlessly in your stomach, causing uneasy churns. Your knees wobble, weakened by adrenaline and the weight of anticipation. Thoughts race through your mind, a jumble of fears and doubts, making it hard to find clarity. Your legs feel heavy as if glued to the ground. The noise of the crowd envelops you, overwhelming your senses. Amidst this whirlwind of emotions, focusing becomes a challenging task, slipping from your grasp like a fleeting breeze.

Well, this has happened to most of us. So, what to do? -- Well, you prepare for it. Here are five ways to prepare yourself for the pressure of competition:

1. Embrace the fear

Stand tall, for fear is a companion of the courageous. Acknowledge the trembling within you, and let it fuel your determination. Embrace the pounding heart and the racing pulse, and channel them into a fiery resolve. While you may not be able to control your stressors, you can always choose your response and your attitude. Nerves and self-doubt are normal; they are your body's way of telling you it is alert, energized and ready to perform.

Instead of battling against the surge of nervous energy, transform it into raw power. Feel the adrenaline coursing through your veins, turning anxiety into a potent fuel. Let it propel you forward, unleashing your full potential.

2. Visualize Triumph

CLOSE YOUR EYES and paint vivid pictures of triumphant moments. Envision yourself conquering every obstacle, standing on that podium, basking in the adulation of victory. Let these visions ignite a fire within, burning away any doubt.

To make visualization work, close your eyes and imagine the physical movements you would make to succeed in competition. Imagine yourself moving at the same speed as you would in real life. Also, make sure you're imagining from your perspective — not from that of an observer. You should be viewing the scene (the crowd, the field) as you would if you were there — not watching yourself compete from the bleachers.

If going to an empty football field and sitting on the bench helps you make the imagined experience more authentic, by all means do so. If the crowd's noise is likely to distract you during a competition, see if you can find an audio recording with crowd noises that you can play while you visualize the event.

Imagine what you see, hear, smell, taste and feel. Using all five senses can help create a powerful image. Whatever you can do to make the imagined experience feel real will aid in translating what you imagine into what you achieve.

3. Breathe with Purpose

INHALE DEEPLY, drawing in strength, and exhale slowly, releasing tension. Harness the power of intentional breaths to calm the storm within you. Let each breath remind you of your ability to find inner calm amidst the chaos.

Relaxation techniques help reduce the physical symptoms of anxiety, such as an increased heart rate, tense muscles, and quick and shallow breathing. These techniques can be used any time before a performance or competition. They may be beneficial when practiced the night before or in the hours preceding an event to help keep nerves at bay.

Finding an absorbing activity like reading a gripping novel or watching an exciting film will stop you from overthinking the event or worrying excessively. Activities like this can be mentally refreshing and bring you to the starting line feeling excited and ready to perform.

4. Use Positive Affirmations

BANISH SELF-DOUBT by drawing from a mental toolbox of positive affirmations that empower you. These are statements you can either run through in your head or say out loud, such as "I can do this," "No one can stop me," I am better, stronger and smarter than the other guy or girl," etc. Repeat these empowering statements to yourself, proclaiming your strength, skill and unwavering determination. Let the power of your words fortify and strengthen your self-belief, driving away any lingering doubts that may arise.

Let the power of your words fortify your self-belief. When nerves threaten to consume you, bring your mind back to the present moment. Tune out distractions and become laser-focused on the task at hand.

Allow the intensity of your concentration to drown out the noise of anxiety, creating a space where you can perform at your absolute best. With each deep breath, inhale confidence and exhale any remnants of doubt or fear.

Embrace the belief that you can achieve greatness and reach your goals. Remind yourself of the obstacles you have already overcome and the victories you have celebrated along your journey. Let these reminders serve as a testament to your resilience and unwavering spirit.

As you face challenges, remember that you possess the strength and determination to overcome them. Embrace each obstacle as an opportunity for growth and learning, knowing that every experience, whether positive or negative, contributes to your personal development. Trust in your abilities and remind yourself that you are more than capable of rising above any adversity.

5. Trust Your Training

REMEMBER, we don't rise to the challenge; we fall to the level of our training. In the face of nervousness, lean on your training for strength. Remember the countless hours of sweat, sacrifice and dedication poured into your preparation. Trust in the strength you have built, for it will carry you through the storm.

Immediately before an event, rest is vital. Resist the temptation to squeeze in more training, hoping a final training session will help on competition day. Training takes time to have an effect, and last-minute exertion is more likely to tire you out than make you perform better. If you are well-rested, you are more likely to perform well.

SUMMARY

Mastering the competition mindset is essential for athletes to unlock their full potential and achieve peak performance during competitions. Most underperformance in sports can be attributed to a lack of mental preparation. Therefore, it is paramount to understand the importance of a competitive mindset and to implement strategies that cultivate it.

A competition mindset refers to athletes' mental approach to performing at their best during competitions. It involves having a performance mindset that focuses on winning through preparation (mental and physical), having a plan (strategy), tuning out distractions and staying present in the moment. Cultivating a performance mindset can be achieved, but you will need the training mindset first.

Strategies for preparing for competition play a crucial role in developing and maintaining the competition mindset. Visualization techniques help athletes mentally rehearse their performances, thus enhancing focus, confidence and overall performance. Positive self-talk is an empowering tool to reinforce belief, manage emotions, and stay motivated.

While stress is often viewed negatively, a small amount can benefit performance by triggering heightened alertness and focus. Learning to manage stress and harness its positive aspects is vital for athletes. Creating a conducive pre-event environment, including proper nutrition and a supportive team, sets you up for optimal performance.

Managing stress and nerves during competition is another critical aspect of mastering the competition mindset. Strategies such as deep breathing, positive visualization, and focusing on the present moment help athletes stay calm, centered, and in control of their performance. By developing effective coping mechanisms and embracing a confident mindset, athletes can overcome pre-competition nervousness and perform at their best when it matters most.

Mastering the competition mindset requires deliberate mental preparation and the implementation of specific strategies. By cultivating a performance mindset, preparing effectively for competition, and managing stress and nerves, young athletes can elevate their performance and unlock their true potential. The competition mindset empowers athletes to embrace challenges, persevere through adversity, and consistently deliver their best performances, ultimately leading to long-term success in their chosen sport.

The competition mindset is focused on winning, but if we get even more specific, it focuses on winning each moment. You have the best chance to win by staying present in each moment. Winning, however, is not guaranteed. To reach the top, you will most definitely fail. If you've ever heard the saying "Failure is not an option," I want you to wipe that from your mind; it is unrealistic. Failure is inevitable, and how far you make it in your sport will be determined by your response to the failure you will face. You won't go far if you allow it to demotivate and discourage you. If you see failure as feedback and use it as fuel, there is no limit to your growth. So, let's learn how to **turn failure into fuel**.

CHAPTER 7
USING FAILURE TO FUEL SUCCESS

MENTAL TOUGHNESS
AND CONFIDENCE

"I have not failed. I've just found 10,000 ways that won't work."

— *Thomas Edison*

Failure is an inevitable part of life, yet it is often met with fear, disappointment and a sense of inadequacy. Embracing failure as a valuable learning opportunity can lead to personal growth, resilience and success. Whether it's a setback in sports or in life, learning to become more comfortable with failure can be a transformative experience.

By shifting your perspective and adopting a growth mindset, you can overcome failure and use it to achieve your goals and aspirations.

Why is Failure Important in the Learning Process?

FAILURE CAN BE DEFINED as the lack of success in achieving a desired outcome or goal. It is a state or condition where one's efforts or actions do not produce the intended or expected results. Failure is often associated with disappointment, frustration or setback.

Failure can occur in various aspects of life, such as personal relationships, education, career, business ventures, or any pursuit that involves setting objectives. Depending on the goal's context and significance, it can manifest as minor setbacks or significant disappointments.

It's important to note that failure is a subjective concept and can be interpreted differently by individuals. While some may view failure as a permanent and adverse outcome, others see it as a valuable learning experience or an opportunity for growth and improvement.

Failure is an inherent part of the human experience, and many successful individuals and organizations have faced failures along their journeys but used them as valuable lessons to adapt, learn and eventually achieve their goals.

You should adopt a positive mindset for failure, seeing it as an opportunity to learn, grow and refine one's approach. Embracing failure as a natural part of the learning process can help you develop resilience, perseverance and the ability to bounce back from setbacks.

You need to understand the value of failing. Failing will help you develop resilience and mental toughness, which are essential for success in sports and life. When you face setbacks and failures, it's an opportunity for you to learn how to bounce back, persevere and maintain a positive mindset despite challenges. This resilience will help you deal with future obstacles and setbacks more effectively.

Failure is the ultimate feedback. It pinpoints what you need to work on. Instead of being discouraged by failure, see it as a chance to grow and refine your skills. Analyze your mistakes, identify areas for development, and seek feedback. By doing so, you'll be able to learn and continuously improve.

You will often face high-pressure situations in sports; failure is part of that experience. Coping with failure early on will help you to better handle pressure and adversity. Stay focused, maintain composure and perform at your best even in challenging circumstances.

Failing also contributes to your character development. It teaches you humility, sportsmanship and the importance of perseverance. Understand that success is not guaranteed and that hard work is necessary to achieve your goals. Be gracious in defeat and respectful of your opponents.

Failing can be a motivating factor for setting realistic goals, working harder, and striving for improvement. When you experience setbacks, it's an opportunity to reassess your strategies, set new objectives and stay committed to your athletic pursuits. Let failure ignite a fire within you to prove yourself and achieve greater success in the future.

Remember, embracing failure as a learning experience will equip you with essential life skills. It will help you become a resilient individual who is not discouraged by setbacks.

WHAT CAN ATHLETES LEARN FROM FAILURES?

Resilience and Mental Toughness

The faster you learn to change your perspective on failure, the quicker you will develop resilience and mental toughness. When you learn from failure, you will improve quicker and see it for what it really is. Failure is feedback. It is feedback in its purest form. Moving past failure becomes much easier when you change your perspective this way. Remember, failure isn't the goal, but it is part of the process.

Take the example of Babe Ruth, one of the greatest baseball players of all time. Despite striking out more than any other player in Major League Baseball, he didn't let it define him. Instead, he learned from his failures and focused on hitting home runs. Babe Ruth's ability to rise above his failures led him to hit 714 home runs. Analyze, adapt and use failure as a tool to become a better athlete.

Increased Self-awareness

FAILURES CAN LEAD athletes to reflect on their strengths and weaknesses, enabling them to identify areas for improvement and focus their efforts more effectively. Failures have a unique way of teaching us about ourselves and our capabilities. When faced with setbacks, it's important to use them as opportunities for self-reflection and increased self-awareness. Take the time to analyze your performance and identify your strengths and weaknesses. Understand that failures can provide valuable insights into areas where you need improvement. By recognizing your weaknesses, you can focus your efforts more effectively.

Use failures as a catalyst to develop a deeper understanding of your capabilities. Reflect on what went wrong and why. Be honest with yourself and learn the lessons that failures offer. Identify patterns or recurring challenges that hinder your progress.

Remember that self-awareness is not about dwelling on your shortcomings or feeling discouraged. It's about embracing your areas for improvement with a growth mindset. See each failure as an opportunity to learn and grow rather than a reflection of your worth as an athlete. Channel your energy into constructive self-assessment and commit to making the necessary changes to overcome your weaknesses.

Ultimately, increased self-awareness will empower you to make better decisions, develop more effective strategies, and reach your full potential as an athlete.

Humility and Sportsmanship

HUMILITY AND SPORTSMANSHIP are essential qualities that every athlete should cultivate, and failures play a significant role in their development. When faced with defeat, it is better to have humility and showcase graciousness in the face of adversity. Remember that true strength lies not only in victory but also in how you handle defeat.

Failures have a way of humbling us, reminding us that there is always room for improvement and growth. They teach us that no matter how talented or skilled we may be, there will always be challenges and opponents who can push us beyond our limits. Accept these moments of humility as opportunities to learn and develop as an athlete and an individual.

Respect for your opponents is another vital aspect of sportsmanship that failures can teach you. Recognize and appreciate the efforts and skills of your adversaries, even in defeat. Understand that competition is not just about winning but also about valuing the spirit of fair play, camaraderie and mutual respect. Treat your opponents with dignity and congratulate them on their successes, regardless of the outcome.

Through failures, you will learn that success is not solely defined by winning but by the integrity and sportsmanship you display on and off the field. Use these experiences as reminders to stay grounded, to remain respectful, and to always uphold the values of fair play.

Remember, as an athlete, you are not just representing yourself but also your team, your coaches and your supporters. Showcasing humility and sportsmanship in both victory and defeat will earn you the admiration and respect of others. It will also contribute to your personal growth and development as a well-rounded athlete.

So, look at failures as opportunities to cultivate humility, demonstrate graciousness in defeat, and foster a deep sense of respect for your opponents. Let your actions on and off the field reflect the values of sportsmanship, and you will become a better athlete and a role model for others.

Character Development

OVERCOMING FAILURES DEVELOPS an athlete's character, instilling qualities such as perseverance, patience, and a positive attitude. Character development is an integral part of your athletic journey, and overcoming failures is a powerful catalyst for growth. Every setback presents an opportunity to cultivate essential qualities that will benefit you as an athlete and a person.

Perseverance is one of the essential virtues that failures instill in you. When faced with challenges and setbacks, developing the ability to persist and keep pushing forward is crucial. Believe that setbacks are temporary road-blocks on your path to success. Stay committed to your goals, maintain a strong work ethic, and refuse to let failures define you. Remember, true champions are not determined by how many times they fall but by how many times they rise after each fall.

Patience is another quality that failures can help you develop. Athletics is a journey that requires time, dedication, and continuous improvement. Fail-ures remind you that success does not come overnight but through consis-tent effort and a long-term approach. Use these moments to cultivate patience, understanding that progress takes time, and that each failure is an opportunity to learn and grow.

A positive attitude is useful when faced with failures. Adopt a positive mindset instead of dwelling on negativity or succumbing to self-doubt. Maintain optimism and believe in your ability to overcome obstacles. A positive attitude strengthens your resolve and inspires those around you.

Character development through failures goes beyond the realm of athlet-ics. The qualities of perseverance, patience and a positive attitude will benefit you in all aspects of life. They will equip you to face challenges head-on, bounce back from setbacks, and navigate the ups and downs with resilience.

Cultivate perseverance, patience and a positive attitude through every setback. Remember, it's not just about becoming a better athlete but also about becoming a better person. Let your character shine through your actions, and you will leave a lasting impact on and off the field.

HOW TO USE FAILURE AS A LEARNING OPPORTUNITY

Accept failure

Accept failures as a natural part of the learning process and view them as opportunities for growth. Failure is not something to be feared or discouraged by. Instead, I encourage you to consider failure as a valuable learning opportunity. It's essential to accept that failures are a natural part of the learning process in sports and life.

Don't let it discourage you when you experience a failure, whether a missed shot, a lost match, or a mistake during practice. See it as an opportunity to learn and develop. Understand that even the greatest athletes have faced failures on their path to success.

Take the time to reflect on the failure and try to understand what went wrong and why. Was it a technical error? Did you lack focus or preparation? Analyze the situation objectively and identify the areas that need improvement.

Seek feedback from your coaches, teammates, and even opponents. They may provide different perspectives and insights that can help you gain a better understanding of the failure. Be open to their feedback and use it constructively to improve your performance.

Once you've identified the areas for improvement, create an action plan. Set specific goals and develop strategies to address the weaknesses you've identified. Work closely with your coaches to design training sessions that target these areas and put in the necessary effort to make progress.

Remember, failure doesn't reflect your worth or potential as an athlete. Instead, it's a progression of becoming better. Maintain a positive attitude and growth mindset. Use failures as fuel to motivate you to work harder and strive for continuous improvement.

By embracing failure as a learning opportunity, you'll develop resilience, determination and a strong sense of self-awareness. You'll become more equipped to handle challenges and setbacks that come your way. Trust the process, stay committed and keep pushing yourself. Remember, failure is not the end—it's an opportunity for growth.

Analyze the Situation

TAKE time to reflect on the failure and objectively assess what went wrong and why. When you encounter a failure, it's essential to take the time to analyze the situation. This means stepping back and reflecting on the failure calmly and objectively. Avoid letting emotions or frustration cloud your judgment. Instead, approach it with a clear and focused mindset.

Ask yourself what went wrong and why it happened. Was it a technical mistake, a lapse in concentration, or a poor decision? By objectively assessing the situation, you can gain valuable insights into the specific factors that contributed to the failure.

During this analysis, be honest with yourself. It's important to take ownership of your mistakes and shortcomings. This self-awareness is essential for personal growth and improvement as an athlete. Recognize that no one is perfect, and failures provide opportunities for learning and development.

Consider seeking input from your coaches, teammates or mentors. They can provide different perspectives and offer valuable feedback on what they observed during the failure. Sometimes, an outside viewpoint can shed light on aspects you have missed.

As you analyze the situation, focus on the process rather than solely on the outcome. Understand that failures can occur even when you've done everything right. Look for patterns or recurring challenges that may be hindering your performance. By identifying these patterns, you can develop strategies to address them effectively.

Remember, the purpose of this analysis is not to dwell on failure or self-blame. Instead, it's about gaining a deeper understanding of what happened and why. This understanding will help you make informed decisions moving forward.

By taking the time to objectively analyze the failure, you can extract valuable lessons from it. These insights will guide you in making the necessary adjustments, refining your skills and ultimately improving your performance.

. . .

Identify areas for improvement

DETERMINE THE SPECIFIC SKILLS, techniques or strategies that need development based on each failure. After analyzing the failure, it's important to identify specific areas for improvement. This step will help you focus your efforts and create a targeted plan for development.

Start by reflecting on the aspects of your performance that directly contributed to the failure. Was it a technical skill that needs refinement? Did you struggle with a particular strategy or decision-making process?

For example, if you missed several shots during a game, you might identify shooting accuracy as an area for improvement. Suppose you struggled with decision-making in a critical moment. You should work on your mental focus and decision-making skills in that case. Be as specific as possible when identifying the areas that need attention.

Consult with your coaches and seek their guidance on the identified areas for improvement. They can provide valuable insight and suggest targeted drills or exercises to enhance the specific skills or techniques you need to develop. Collaborating with your coaches will ensure that you align your efforts with their expertise and the overall team strategy.

Set clear and measurable goals for each area of improvement. Make them specific, realistic and time bound. For example, your goal might be to increase shooting accuracy by a certain percentage within a specified time frame.

Develop a plan of action that outlines the steps you'll take to improve in the identified areas. This may include additional practice sessions, specialized training exercises or seeking extra support and guidance from your coaches or trainers.

Remember that improvement takes time and consistent effort. Don't get discouraged if progress is gradual. Stay focused and motivated, knowing that each small step forward brings you closer to your overall development as an athlete.

By identifying the specific areas for improvement and creating a plan of action, you're taking proactive steps to address the weaknesses revealed by the failure. This targeted approach will help you grow as an athlete and ultimately enhance your performance.

Seek Feedback

ENGAGE WITH COACHES, teammates or mentors to gain different perspectives and valuable insights on improving. Seeking feedback is essential in your journey to improve as an athlete. Engaging with coaches, teammates and mentors will provide you with valuable perspectives and insights that can help you identify blind spots, uncover areas for improvement, and gain a well-rounded understanding of your performance.

First and foremost, make it a habit to actively seek feedback from your coaches. They have the expertise and knowledge to evaluate your performance objectively. Approach them with a genuine desire to learn and improve. Ask specific questions about your strengths, weaknesses, and areas for growth. Their feedback will provide you with valuable guidance and direction.

In addition to coaches, your teammates can also provide valuable feedback. They observe your performance from a different perspective and may have insights that complement your coach's observations. Engage in open and constructive discussions with your teammates. Ask for their honest opinions and suggestions on how you can improve.

Mentors, such as former athletes or experienced individuals, can offer valuable insights based on their experiences. Seek opportunities to connect with them and ask for their guidance. Their perspective can give you a broader understanding and provide practical advice on overcoming challenges and improving your performance.

When receiving feedback, it's crucial to approach it with an open mind and a willingness to learn. Avoid becoming defensive and embrace constructive criticism. Remember, the goal is not to prove yourself right or wrong but to gather insights that will contribute to your growth as an athlete.

Take notes or record feedback to ensure that you can refer to it later. Analyze the feedback objectively and identify common themes or patterns. This will help you gain a clear understanding of the areas that require your attention and provide a basis for developing an action plan.

You gain multiple perspectives on your performance by actively seeking feedback from coaches, teammates, and mentors. This diverse feedback will enable you to develop a well-rounded approach to your improvement.

Create an Action Plan

SET specific goals and develop a plan of action to address the identified areas for improvement. Creating an action plan is essential in utilizing feedback and turning it into tangible progress. By setting specific goals and developing a plan of action, you'll have a clear roadmap for addressing the identified areas for improvement. Here's how you can create an effective action plan:

Based on the feedback and your assessment, set goals based on the key elements discussed in this book. Divide each goal into smaller, manageable steps. This will make your action plan more approachable and help you track progress.

Determine the specific tasks or actions that must be undertaken to achieve each step of your goals. For instance, if your goal is to enhance form, actionable tasks could include studying video tutorials, practicing proper shooting techniques with a coach and incorporating form drills into your training routine.

Regularly assess your progress, track your improvements, note any challenges you encounter, and adjust your action plan as necessary. This monitoring will help you stay accountable and make necessary adjustments along the way.

Developing an action plan gives you a roadmap that directs your efforts toward specific goals. It provides structure, accountability and a clear path for improvement. Remember, consistent effort and dedication to your action plan will lead to noticeable progress over time.

. . .

Learn from Mistakes

UNDERSTAND the lessons learned from the failure and avoid making the same errors in future situations. Learning from your mistakes is vital to your growth as an athlete. It allows you to understand the lessons learned from failure and avoid repeating the same errors in future situations. Here's how you can effectively learn from your mistakes:

Take the time to reflect on the failure and clearly understand what went wrong. Analyze the situation, your actions and the outcomes. Identify the specific mistakes or errors that contributed to the failure.

Dig deep to understand the underlying reasons behind the mistakes. Was it a lack of preparation, poor decision-making or a technical flaw? By identifying the root causes, you can address them directly and prevent similar mistakes from occurring again.

Consider the lessons you've learned from the failure. Reflect on how the failure has impacted your performance, mindset or approach to the sport. Use these lessons as valuable knowledge for future situations.

Based on the lessons learned, make the necessary adjustments to your approach. Modify your training routine, refine your techniques or develop strategies to overcome specific challenges. Adapt your approach to align with the lessons learned and set yourself up for success in the future.

Don't hesitate to seek guidance and support from your coaches, teammates or mentors. Share the lessons you've learned and ask for their insights and advice. Their experience and expertise can provide valuable guidance to help you avoid repeating the same mistakes.

You can grow, evolve and become a better athlete by learning from your mistakes. Apply the lessons you've learned to future situations, ensuring you avoid making the same errors.

SUMMARY

Failure is an integral part of the learning process for young athletes. It catalyzes the development of mental toughness, resilience and a growth mindset. By understanding the importance of failure and learning how to use it as a valuable learning opportunity, athletes can unlock their full potential and pave their way to success.

Failure provides helpful feedback and teaches athletes essential lessons about their strengths, weaknesses and areas for improvement. It challenges them to reassess their strategies, techniques and approaches, leading to growth and refinement. Embracing failure allows athletes to develop the resilience needed to bounce back from setbacks and the determination to persevere through challenges.

Learning from failure requires a mindset shift. Athletes must view failure as an opportunity for growth and learning rather than a reflection of their worth or abilities. They should seek feedback, analyze their mistakes and adjust their training and performance accordingly. By doing so, they can continuously evolve and improve.

Strategies such as reflecting on failures, seeking guidance, setting incremental goals and implementing changes are instrumental in using failure as a learning opportunity. These strategies foster self-awareness, adaptability and a proactive approach to personal growth. With the right mindset and strategy, athletes can transform setbacks into success.

Ultimately, the ability to accept failure and use it as a catalyst for growth sets athletes apart. It cultivates a mindset that values perseverance, continuous improvement, and the courage to take risks. Failure becomes fuel for success, a necessary component of the journey to achieving greatness.

I encourage you to accept failure, learn from it and continuously strive to improve. Take on the challenges and setbacks as opportunities for growth, knowing that each failure brings you closer to your goals. With a resilient spirit and a growth mindset, you have the power to overcome any obstacle and achieve greatness in your athletic pursuits. Believe in yourself and the learning process, and let failure propel you toward the success you deserve.

Mental toughness is essential not only in sports but in life as well. It will enable you to handle high-pressure situations, adapt to change and turn setbacks into comebacks. Let's look at some real-life examples of people who have used their mindset to beat the odds.

CHAPTER 8
MENTAL TOUGHNESS IN THE REAL WORLD

MENTAL TOUGHNESS
AND CONFIDENCE

"Those who have a 'why' to live, can bear with almost any 'how'."

— Viktor Frankl

MY STORY

I reported to BUD/s weighing 135 pounds and had never been in the ocean or run farther than a mile and a half; I became a SEAL one rock at a time. Growing up, I was much smaller than the other kids, so I had to work twice as hard to get my spot. When 9/11 happened, I had just finished high school and planned to play college golf. I was born in Texas and raised to love this country, and I felt called to serve.

Even though I didn't know anyone who died on that tragic day, golf did not seem important. A day or two later, I went to the recruiting office. I was clueless about what branches did what or even what the jobs were, but I had heard something about SEALs and them being the best, so I went to the Navy office first. To put it nicely, the Navy recruiter was not in the best shape and claimed that he had worked with SEALs. Unimpressed, I went to the Marine Corps office next door. There sat two men who looked like they could kill me with one finger. This impressed me and I signed up.

Surprisingly, I was denied entry due to a perceived medical limitation. When I was 13, I broke my arm and had to get a titanium plate put in it. Not only did it disqualify me from the Marine Corps but all the other branches as well. I asked the recruiter what I could do, and he said I could wait 18-24 months and apply for a waiver. But in the meantime, I would have to find something else to do.

I worked various jobs and attempted college, but I lacked purpose. I had heard the call, but my dreams had been smashed. So, I waited. During this time, I started researching the different special operations units, and I knew without a doubt that I wanted to be a SEAL. When I told people, they laughed at me. This only made me want it more; however I did not say a word. I just decided to show them. Actions speak louder than words.

Long story short, my waiver was approved and I enlisted in the Navy under the SEAL challenge program. When I showed up to BUD/s, there were Olympic-caliber athletes there with me, and in the back of my mind I was thinking, "How am I possibly going to compete with these guys?" By the end of the training, I was winning the four-mile timed runs. This happened because; 1) I got stronger and faster, and 2) everyone faster than me quit during hell week.

Hell Week is renowned for being the hardest part of the most challenging military training on earth. I made through one rock at a time. It didn't matter how tired I was; I just focused on a rock 10 feet in front of me. I repeated this process for a week. It's really that simple. If you're going to accomplish something hard, pick the thing right in front of you and forget about everything else, then repeat.

After the Navy, I chased my PGA tour dream for three years. I had the best coaches and sponsors. I did public speaking and security contracting, and I was even a 5-star Uber driver. I was willing to do whatever it took to chase my dream. The third time I ran out of money, I knew it was time for a change. My family had sacrificed enough. So, I started looking for a job.

After 100 job applications and 20 interviews, still no job. My confidence was shattered, and I became depressed. Where had the kid that had made it through Hell Week gone? After a couple of weeks, I snapped out of it, or maybe my wife snapped me out of it. It was time for a self-assessment.

I realized I needed to learn new skills and how the skills I already had applied to the business world. I needed to learn a new language. I was also on a short timeline. I found a business school that was focused on entrepreneurship and taught by successful entrepreneurs; however, they had started two weeks prior. I refused to accept this answer and got the CEO of the school on the phone to plead my case. I told him that if he gave me a chance, I would not only catch up, I would outwork everyone there.

He let me in. I worked 20-hour days with no sleep, no rest. With discipline, focus, and attention to detail, I learned to ask the right questions and recognize patterns. I gained the skills and finished top of my class. By the end of the year, I had 15 job offers. What a difference a year can make.

Mental toughness isn't a one-time thing; you will need it for the rest of your life. If you lose it, don't worry. You can get it back; reboot the system, starting with an honest self-assessment, and then get after it.

PARALLELS BETWEEN MENTAL TOUGHNESS IN SPORTS AND LIFE

Mental toughness is not limited to sports. It permeates every aspect of your life, equipping you with the resilience, discipline, and growth mindset needed to excel academically, professionally and personally. By cultivating mental toughness, you will become better equipped to face challenges and seize life's opportunities.

Resilience

LET'S talk about the parallels between mental toughness in sports and life, specifically focusing on resilience. Resilience plays a vital role in sports. It is the ability to bounce back from setbacks, to stay focused and motivated even in the face of adversity. Athletes face numerous obstacles such as injuries, losses or performance slumps. Recovering from poor performance is essential for an athlete's success. The mentally tough ones can quickly recover from such setbacks and continue pushing forward.

For example, imagine a young soccer player who misses a penalty kick during a game. A mentally tough athlete would acknowledge the disappointment but then use it as fuel to work harder, practice more, and improve their skills for the next opportunity. However, when athletes excessively dwell on their failures, it adversely affects their performance.

You must focus on the present moment and concentrate on the current task. It becomes challenging to do so when the mind is consumed by an error that happened three plays ago.

The same qualities that help you develop resilience in sports can be applied to challenges beyond the field. In sports and life, resilience is built through a combination of mindset, self-belief, and determination.

To strengthen your resilience, focus on three key areas. First, develop a growth mindset where you view failures and setbacks as opportunities for learning and improvement rather than as signs of inadequacy. Take on challenges and see them as a chance to grow stronger.

Second, build belief in yourself and trust your abilities, skills and training. Remind yourself of the successes you've achieved and the obstacles you've overcome before.

Third, perseverance is the key to staying committed to your goals. Work harder, even when faced with difficulties. Keep pushing forward, adapting your approach if needed, and never give up. It's through perseverance that you build mental toughness both in sports and in life.

Being resilient is not natural but a skill you can learn and develop over time. By applying these principles in sports and life, you'll be better equipped to overcome challenges and achieve your goals. Stay resilient, believe in yourself, and keep pushing forward on and off the field.

Goal setting

THE PARALLELS between sports and life regarding goal setting lie in the principles and benefits it offers. In both cases, goal setting provides clarity, direction, and motivation. It helps individuals prioritize their efforts, break down large objectives into smaller achievable tasks, and measure progress.

Positive Mindset

A POSITIVE MINDSET is a powerful tool that can significantly impact performance and well-being. In sports, maintaining a positive mindset is necessary for high performance. It involves cultivating an optimistic outlook, focusing on strengths and possibilities, and managing negative thoughts or self-doubt. Athletes who maintain a positive mindset can handle pressure, stay motivated, and bounce back from setbacks. For example, a basketball player who misses an easy shot can maintain a positive mindset by focusing on the next opportunity to contribute to the team's success instead of dwelling on the mistake.

Maintaining a positive mindset is essential in overcoming stress and challenges in everyday life. Life often presents us with unexpected difficulties and maintaining a positive outlook can help you navigate them effectively. A positive mindset allows you to approach stressors with resilience, optimism and a problem-solving attitude. It enables you to find silver linings, learn from experiences, and maintain emotional well-being. For instance, when facing a challenging situation at work or school, maintaining a positive mindset can help you view it as an opportunity for growth and finding creative solutions.

The parallels between sports and life in terms of positivity lie in its impact on our mental and emotional well-being. A positive mindset in sports and everyday life allows us to build resilience, improve overall performance, and maintain a healthy perspective.

To cultivate a positive mindset, focus on positive self-talk. Replace self-criticism or negative thoughts with positive and encouraging affirmations. Remind yourself of your strengths, past successes, and ability to overcome challenges.

Practice gratitude. Take time each day to reflect on the things you are grateful for. This helps shift your focus to the positive aspects of your life and cultivates a sense of appreciation.

Remember that maintaining a positive mindset is a choice and a skill that can be developed over time. By consistently practicing these strategies in sports and everyday life, you will strengthen your ability to maintain a positive outlook, overcome stress, and achieve your goals.

Teamwork

TEAMWORK REFERS to the collaborative effort of individuals working together towards a common goal. It involves effective communication, mutual support, and coordinating and synchronizing actions with teammates. Teams that prioritize teamwork are often more successful because they can leverage each member's strengths, cover for weaknesses, and achieve a level of synergy that individual efforts alone cannot produce. To be an effective teammate on and off the field, you should have self-discipline, good communication, and decision-making skills.

Teamwork is essential in various aspects of life. Whether in the workplace, school projects, or personal relationships, working well with others and collaborating towards a shared objective is essential. In the workplace, individuals who excel at teamwork can contribute their unique skills and ideas, support their colleagues, and foster a positive and productive work environment. Collaboration allows students to pool their strengths, share knowledge, and achieve better outcomes in school. Even in personal relationships, teamwork is vital in creating harmony, resolving conflicts, and supporting each other's goals and aspirations.

Both in sports and everyday life, teamwork enhances productivity, fosters creativity, builds trust, and strengthens relationships. By working together, individuals can accomplish more, overcome obstacles, and celebrate collective success.

To foster teamwork, I encourage you to focus on effective communication. Listen actively to your teammates, express your thoughts clearly, and provide constructive feedback. Good communication helps avoid misunderstandings, aligns everyone's efforts and strengthens relationships.

EXAMPLES OF MENTAL TOUGHNESS

Here are some great examples of people who initially suffered failure but overcame it due to their mental toughness and became hugely successful.

Before becoming successful with the Harry Potter series, J.K. Rowling faced numerous rejections from publishers before becoming one of the most successful authors of all time. She was even advised to get a day job because there was little chance of her making a living through writing. However, she persevered and eventually found a publisher who believed in her work.

Matt Biondi's story is a perfect example of mental toughness and the power of a comeback. Despite starting the 1988 Olympic Games with two losses, the champion swimmer demonstrated resilience, determination and mental strength to bounce back and win five gold medals. Biondi could have easily been discouraged or allowed the setbacks to affect his performance and confidence. However, his mental toughness enabled him to stay focused, learn from his mistakes and channel his disappointment into renewed motivation. Instead of dwelling on the losses, he used them as fuel to push himself even harder.

Danielle Ballengee's story is a remarkable example of mental toughness. She spent two days stranded after falling down a 60-foot cliff and enduring a shattered pelvis and internal bleeding. Despite the challenges, she recovered and, within 150 days, finished fifth in a 60-mile adventure race that included various demanding activities. Her journey highlights the power of mental resilience, determination, and refusal to be defined by setbacks. Ballengee's story serves as an inspiration, demonstrating that with mental toughness, one can overcome extreme adversity and achieve extraordinary feats.

The co-founder of Apple Inc. faced setbacks early in his career. After developing the Macintosh computer, Steve Jobs was ousted from his company in 1985. Undeterred, he went on to establish other successful ventures including NeXT Inc., which was later acquired by Apple and ultimately led to his triumphant return to the company and the creation of iconic products like the iPod, iPhone and iPad.

Roger Federer is widely regarded as the greatest tennis player in history. Despite his incredible success, Federer faced setbacks early in his career. For three consecutive years, he experienced defeat in the first round of Wimbledon, one of the most prestigious tennis tournaments. However, he displayed mental toughness by staying committed to his game. This mental toughness allowed Federer to bounce back from those early defeats and win seven Wimbledon titles.

The renowned author of horror and suspense novels, Stephen King, had his fair share of rejection early on. His first novel, "Carrie," was rejected by over 30 publishers. Feeling discouraged, he even threw the manuscript away, but his wife retrieved it and convinced him to give it another shot. It eventually found a publisher, becoming a bestseller and launching King's prolific career.

Harland David Sanders, the founder of Kentucky Fried Chicken (KFC), faced numerous failures throughout his life. He held various jobs, including a failed law career and running a gas station, before starting KFC in his late 40s. Despite receiving over 1,000 rejections when trying to sell his fried chicken recipe, Sanders persisted and eventually succeeded with the KFC franchise.

Before becoming a renowned fashion designer, Vera Wang pursued a career as a professional figure skater. However, after failing to make the U.S. Olympic team, she shifted her focus to fashion. Despite facing initial rejections and being told she was too old to break into the industry, Wang persevered and became a prominent designer known for her elegant bridal gowns.

These stories demonstrate that setbacks happen to almost everyone. Still, those with mental toughness ride the storm successfully and reach great heights in their endeavor.

STRATEGIES FOR BUILDING MENTAL TOUGHNESS IN ALL AREAS OF LIFE

Building mental toughness is an essential characteristic that can positively impact all areas of your life. Here are several strategies that can help you develop mental toughness:

Keep a Journal

JOURNALING IS an effective and underrated solution for strengthening mental toughness. Writing down daily reflections, gratitude or challenges can improve self-awareness and provide a sense of perspective. It allows you to track progress, identify patterns and develop a resilient mindset by focusing on solutions and growth.

Write a letter to yourself

WRITE yourself a letter about why you want to achieve whatever you're trying to achieve. When you're feeling discouraged, read the letter. I had a list of all the people who told me I would never be a SEAL, and when I was low on motivation, I read that letter.

Encourage yourself

IMAGINE what you would say to a close friend facing a difficult or stressful situation. When you are in a similar situation, direct those compassionate responses toward yourself. Offer yourself words of encouragement and support.

Get Out of Your Comfort Zone

We stay in our comfort zone to avoid feelings of anxiety or stress, and pain. Anything outside our comfort zone creates uncertainty, making us anxious. Naturally, human beings are programmed to avoid these feelings. This makes them reluctant to leave their comfort zone.

Regularly stepping outside of your comfort zone helps build mental toughness by exposing you to new challenges and unfamiliar situations. You need to be comfortable being uncomfortable.

Here are 5 ways to get out of your comfort zone:

1. Talk to new people. Challenge yourself to strike up a conversation with someone you don't know. This can help you overcome social anxiety and broaden your social connections.
2. Every day is a new learning experience. Embrace a growth mindset and seek opportunities to learn something new each day. By actively seeking knowledge and experiences, you expand your comfort zone and develop new skills.
3. Compliment people. Challenge yourself to express genuine compliments to others. Make it a habit to acknowledge and appreciate people's qualities or achievements. Complimenting others helps you step out of your comfort zone by initiating positive interactions, fostering a sense of connection, and uplifting others.
4. Take on a fitness challenge. Push your physical limits and challenge yourself with a fitness goal that pushes you out of your comfort zone. It could be running a marathon, trying a new intense workout class, or participating in a challenging obstacle course race. By committing to a fitness challenge, you not only improve your physical health but also build resilience and mental strength.
5. Choose a Fear and Face It. Identify a specific fear that holds you back and actively work on conquering it. It could be fear of public

speaking, heights or spiders. Gradually expose yourself to the fear in controlled situations, seeking support and guidance if needed. As you confront and overcome your fears, you develop confidence and resilience.

Develop a Daily Routine

Establishing a consistent daily routine provides structure and discipline. It helps in managing time effectively, setting priorities, and maintaining focus.

Creating a daily routine requires careful consideration and prioritization of your needs and goals. Once you clearly understand your priorities, break down your larger goals into smaller, more manageable steps.

To effectively implement your routine, lay out a plan that spans one week at a time. Write down your tasks and appointments on a calendar, treating them as essential commitments. Consistency is key, so aim to establish specific times for your activities.

Tracking your progress is a powerful method to stay accountable. Create a visual calendar and mark off each day you complete your tasks. This visual representation will encourage you to maintain your streak and avoid breaking the chain.

Keep Your Connections Strong

BUILDING AND MAINTAINING positive relationships with family, friends and mentors is necessary for mental toughness. Supportive connections provide encouragement, advice and a sense of belonging. They can offer different perspectives, help navigate challenges, and offer accountability. Strong relationships contribute to emotional resilience and a sense of community.

In today's fast-paced world, intentionally schedule quality time with your loved ones, friends and yourself. Prioritize these moments of connection, and witness how they transform the quality of your relationships and self-awareness. When engaging in conversations, listen with your heart rather than your head. Avoid the urge to formulate responses or interrupt; instead, be fully present.

SUMMARY

Understanding the parallels between mental toughness in sports and life offers valuable insights into the qualities and strategies that can be applied across various areas of one's life. Mental toughness is not limited to the realm of sports; rather, it encompasses a mindset and set of skills that can be harnessed to overcome challenges, achieve goals and navigate the ups and downs of life.

By understanding and harnessing the qualities and strategies inherent in mental toughness, individuals can navigate challenges, cultivate resilience, regulate emotions, set and pursue goals, foster self-belief, maintain discipline, and seek support. Applying these principles across various areas of life can lead to personal growth, improved performance and an enhanced sense of well-being.

CONCLUSION – TIME TO GET STARTED

MENTAL TOUGHNESS
AND CONFIDENCE

"We don't rise to the level of our expectations, we fall to the level of our training."

— Archilochus

This book is your roadmap, guiding you to develop the resilience, confidence and grit needed for success in sports and life. Let's review the core concepts and strategies we have gone through in the book that will transform your mindset and elevate your performance.

Remember, it's not just about the will to win but the will to prepare to win. Mental toughness involves skills like focus, determination, adaptability and emotional control. You must understand that mental toughness is essential; it is the key factor in allowing you to perform your best under pressure, overcome setbacks and stay motivated.

You will start by honestly assessing yourself. To do this, you must understand the critical skills needed in your sport and compare your current skills to these. If you need help assessing yourself, ask for help, but don't get upset if you don't like what you hear. Remember, false confidence is worse than no confidence because false confidence must be broken down before you can build real confidence.

Once you understand what you need to work on, you'll need the knowledge. You'll need a deep understanding of the skill you hope to master before you can turn it into a skill. Use every resource available. This includes coaches, mentors and resources like this book.

Once you have the knowledge, turn it into skill. You'll do this through deliberate practice. Deliberate practice must become the foundation for your training. Remember to start with the easiest skills to master and break them down into small steps; this will let you get little wins and help you build momentum. The training mindset is essential for developing skills. You've been provided with strategies for staying motivated during training, dealing with stress and overcoming barriers.

Mastering the competition mindset is crucial as you step onto the competitive stage. Remember, visualization and positive self-talk have a place but are supplemental to your skills. It is hard to get results from visualizing the execution of a skill you do not possess. So, build the skills and use visualization to focus those skills. Positive self-talk can help, but if you want to be your best under pressure, you must spend more time under pressure. I gave you some tips on how to do that. Remember, pressure is all in your mind. There is no magic formula to eliminate it; you just have to get used to it. If you go in with this mindset, you'll get used to it. You'll even start to like it.

Failure is not something to fear; it's an opportunity for growth. Practice managing failure and use it as a valuable learning tool. Remember, failure is not our goal, but it is to be expected and not avoided. If you are not failing, it means one of two things. First, you are staying in your comfort zone; in this case, start pushing out of your comfort zone. Do something today that is outside your comfort zone. Second, you are the best in the world; in this case, congratulations.

Mental toughness goes beyond sports; it translates to success in all areas of life. We have explored how resilience, goal setting, a positive mindset, and teamwork can be applied in your family, work, and school. Take these invaluable lessons and use them in every area of your life. Unleash the indomitable spirit within you and conquer adversity in all its forms. Let mental toughness be the driving force that propels you towards success and fulfillment, not just on the field but in all your endeavors.

You've seen practical strategies, inspiring stories and actionable advice throughout this book. Remember, developing mental toughness is not an overnight process but with dedication, practice and the guidance provided in the book. You'll become an unbreakable athlete ready to conquer any challenge that comes your way.

Remember that mental toughness is a lifelong pursuit. It's a journey of self-discovery, growth and continuous improvement. Embrace the challenges, setbacks and victories along the way, for they will shape you into a resilient, confident and unbreakable individual.

I encourage you to set your sights on a specific goal for your mental toughness development. Is it mastering a new skill that has eluded you? Overcoming a seemingly insurmountable challenge that stands in your way? Or perhaps elevating your performance to heights never reached? Whatever the dream, dare to dream big and take action now.

Now, armed with this book's knowledge, tools and strategies, go out there and conquer the world. I challenge you to rise above the ordinary and embrace the extraordinary power of mental toughness. Let its fire ignite your spirit, fuel your determination and propel you toward greatness.

Remember, the path to becoming unbreakable is not for the faint of heart. It requires unwavering commitment, relentless dedication and a warrior's mindset. But fear not, for you possess the potential to transform into a force to be reckoned with.

You're on a journey of self-discovery and growth. Meet the challenges head-on, conquer the obstacles and let your unyielding spirit shine through. Believe in yourself, trust the process, and never underestimate the power of mental toughness. You have the potential to achieve greatness both on and off the field. The path to becoming invincible starts now.

CONCLUSION - TIME TO GET STARTED

Go forth and seize the world with the power of your mind, the strength of your will and the fire in your heart. The time is now. The stage is set. Unleash your greatness and become the unstoppable force you were born to be.

JUST ONE CLICK TO HELP ANOTHER ATHLETE!

MENTAL TOUGHNESS
AND CONFIDENCE

As you set out on this journey of personal growth that will help you not just in your sport, but in all areas of life, you're in the perfect position to hand the baton over to someone else.

Simply by sharing your honest opinion of this book, you'll show other young athletes and their coaches where they can find the guidance they need to build the mental fortitude necessary to really see what they're capable of on the field.

Thank you so much for your support. I wish you the best of luck on your journey.

FREE BONUS CONTENT: YOU NEED THIS HACK!

MENTAL TOUGHNESS
AND CONFIDENCE

When I was playing professional golf, I met an Olympic swim coach who showed me a form of visualization that could be used to build skills. He used it with Olympians to break world records. I tried it myself, and it works well. I have created a free bonus chapter explaining how you can implement this method. You can download it with the link below or by scanning the QR code.

https://mentaltoughnessandconfidence.com/visualize-to-actualize/

SCAN ME

OFFERING 1 ON 1 COACHING FOR A LIMITED TIME

MENTAL TOUGHNESS
AND CONFIDENCE

SCAN ME

If you are looking to continue building your mental toughness and confidence, mentaltoughnessandconfidence.com has a wealth of resources. I offer one-on-one coaching for those wanting to elevate their mindset and training. Space is limited, so I only take on the most serious candidates with the drive to succeed. Take advantage of this and book a free call today to see if we're a good fit. Just head to my website and fill out the contact form or shoot me an email.

chad@mentaltoughnessandconfidence.com

JOIN OUR COMMUNITY

MENTAL TOUGHNESS
AND CONFIDENCE

the Facebook Group!

If you enjoyed this book, you are the perfect fit to join our community of athletes, parents and coaches passionate about *Building Young Athletes' Mental Toughness and Confidence.*

Click here to join the Facebook Group! or use the QR code.

After you join, feel free to introduce yourself. I look forward to hearing about your progress and journey as you start building your mindset. See you in

RESOURCES TO HELP YOU IMPLEMENT THE SYSTEM NOW

The first step is often the hardest when learning something new. That's why I have created these accompanying resources. They are laid out to follow the book. I recommend starting with the workbook as you read this book. Once the workbook is completed, you will start your journal (there is an intro to journaling in the workbook).

Workbook

Journal

SOCIAL MEDIA LINKS

Instagram: @chad__metcalf

TikTok: @chad__metcalf

YouTube @chadmetcalf

Spotify - Chad Metcalf

REFERENCES

Athletic Coaching. (n.d.). True Colors International. Retrieved from https://www.truecolorsintl.com/athletic-coaching

Why Are So Many Kids Dropping Out of Sports. (n.d.). Play for Smiles. Retrieved from https://playforsmiles.com/blogs/today-in-youth-sports/112330823-why-are-so-many-kids-dropping-out-of-sports

Bryant, B. (n.d.). Quotes. Right Attitudes. Retrieved from http://inspiration.rightattitudes.com/authors/bear-bryant/

Grit. (n.d.). Health Stuff. Retrieved from https://healthstuff.us/grit/

Vegan Boxers. (n.d.). Punch Prime. Retrieved from https://punchprime.com/vegan-boxers/

Pre-competition nerves: athletes' advice. (n.d.). World Athletics. Retrieved from https://worldathletics.org/personal-best/performance/pre-competition-nerves-anxiety-advice-tips

Slider Base. (n.d.). Retrieved from https://www.sliderbase.com/spitem-353-1.html

Mental Toughness Words. (n.d.). Mental Toughness Partners. Retrieved from https://www.mentaltoughness.partners/mental-toughness-words/

Glossary. (n.d.). Introduction to Psychology. Retrieved from https://openpress.usask.ca/introductiontopsychology/back-matter/glossary/

Do you think mental toughness is inherent or… (n.d.). Reddit. Retrieved from https://www.reddit.com/r/Gymnastics/comments/nx17nk/do_you_think_mental_toughness_is_inherit_or/

What can I do to improve my mental toughness? (n.d.). Reddit. Retrieved from https://www.reddit.com/r/volleyball/comments/2t0kku/what_can_i_do_to_improve_my_mental_toughness/

Training mental toughness. (n.d.). Reddit. Retrieved from https://www.reddit.com/r/crossfit/comments/t72tmp/training_mental_toughness/

r/running, can we talk about mental… (n.d.). Reddit. Retrieved from https://www.reddit.com/r/running/comments/2itwec/rrunning_can_we_talk_about_mental/

Jersey Watch. (n.d.). Uncovering the Reasons Kids Drop Out of Youth Sports. Retrieved from https://www.jerseywatch.com/blog/reasons-kids-drop-out-of-youth-sports

9 Star Athletes Who Have Talked About Mental Health. (n.d.). Sportify It. Retrieved from https://sportifyit.com/9-star-athletes-who-have-talked-about-mental-health/

Mental Toughness Partners. (n.d.). What is mental toughness? Retrieved from https://www.mentaltoughness.partners/what-is-mental-toughness/#:~:text=Mental%20Toughness%20is%20a%20personality,%2C%20resilience%2C%20grit%20and%20perseverance.

Clear, J. (n.d.). The science of developing mental toughness in your health, work, and life. Retrieved from https://jamesclear.com/mental-toughness

Mental Toughness Inc. (n.d.). What is mental toughness? Retrieved from https://www.mentaltoughnessinc.com/what-is-mental-toughness/

Gleeson, B. (2020, June 24). 13 habits of mentally tough people. Forbes. Retrieved from https://www.forbes.com/sites/brentgleeson/2020/06/24/13-habits-of-mentally-tough-people/?sh=16c4fc655d4d\

REFERENCES

Ohio University. (n.d.). The importance of mental toughness. Retrieved from https://online masters.ohio.edu/blog/the-importance-of-mental-toughness/#:~:text=Sports%20can%20en courage%20young%20athletes,%2C%20time%20management%2C%20and%20discipline.

Success Starts Within. (n.d.). How do young athletes develop mental toughness? Retrieved from https://www.successstartswithin.com/blog/how-do-young-athletes-develop-mental-toughness

Trine University. (2021). Mental toughness: The key to athletic success. Retrieved from https://www.trine.edu/academics/centers/center-for-sports-studies/blog/2021/mental_toughness_the_key_to_athletic_success.aspx

Everyday Health. (n.d.). Can getting mentally tough up your game in sports? The answer is yes. Retrieved from https://www.everydayhealth.com/wellness/resilience/can-getting-mentally-tough-up-your-game-sports-answer-yes/

Human Performance Resource Center. (n.d.). 7 myths and facts about mental toughness. Retrieved from https://www.hprc-online.org/mental-fitness/performance-psychology/7-myths-and-facts-about-mental-toughness

South Bay Community Services. (n.d.). Debunking myths about mental strength. Retrieved from https://www.southbaycommunityservices.com/debunking-myths-about-mental-strength/

Sport Psychology Today. (n.d.). The top myths that prevent athletes from embracing mental training. Retrieved from https://www.sportpsychologytoday.com/youth-sports-psychol ogy/the-top-myths-that-prevent-athletes-from-embracing-mental-training/

Queen's University. (n.d.). Self-Assessment. Retrieved from https://www.queensu.ca/teachin gandlearning/modules/assessments/25_s3_03_self_assessment.html

Skills Shark. (n.d.). Athlete self-assessments. Retrieved from https://skillshark.com/athlete-self-assessments/

Nova Southeastern University. (n.d.). View content. Retrieved from https://nsuworks.nova. edu/cgi/viewcontent.cgi?article=3737&context=tqr

Warrior Mind Coach. (n.d.). Improving athletic performance through self-evaluation. Retrieved from https://www.warriormindcoach.com/improving-athletic-performance-through-self-evaluation/

Mac, B. (n.d.). iSEQ. Retrieved from https://www.brianmac.co.uk/iseq.htm

AUT Millennium. (n.d.). 50 questions. Retrieved from https://news.autmillennium.org.nz/athlete-development/50-questions/

Springer. (2020). An updated review of the efficacy of eating disorder prevention programs. Retrieved from https://link.springer.com/article/10.1007/s40279-020-01299-4

Parkin, G. (n.d.). Why assessment is fundamental for young athlete development. Retrieved from https://www.linkedin.com/pulse/why-assessment-fundamental-young-athlete-development-guy-parkin

Precision Athletica. (n.d.). The importance of screening young athletes. Retrieved from https://www.precisionathletica.com.au/importance-of-screening-young-athletes/

Human Kinetics. (n.d.). Assessing your athlete. Retrieved from https://us.humankinetics. com/blogs/excerpt/assessing-your-athlete

EdApp. (n.d.). 10 skills assessment tools. Retrieved from https://www.edapp.com/blog/10-skills-assessment-tools/

PE Office. (n.d.). Why performance analysis is important for development in sport. Retrieved from https://blog.peoffice.co.uk/why-performance-analysis-is-important-for-develop ment-in-sport/

Clearinghouse for Sport. (n.d.). Performance Analysis. Retrieved from https://www.clearing houseforsport.gov.au/kb/performance-analysis

National Academy of Sports Medicine. (n.d.). Sports Performance Testing & Evaluation: A Whole Team Approach. Retrieved from https://blog.nasm.org/sports-performance/ sports-performance-testing-evaluation-whole-team-approach

Metrifit. (n.d.). Coach feedback: How important is it? Retrieved from https://metrifit.com/ blog/coach-feedback-how-important-is-it/#:~:text=Feedback%20is%20a%20critical% 20component%20of%20coaching&text=Feedback%20allows%20coaches%20to% 20tell,Schwandt%20%26%20Bartz%2C%201990).

Chicago State University. (n.d.). Guide to coaching and feedback. Retrieved from https:// www.csu.edu/humanresources/empdev/documents/GuidetoCoachingandFeedback.pdf

Youth Sports Psychology. (n.d.). The importance of positive feedback for young athletes. Retrieved from https://www.youthsportspsychology.com/youth_sports_psycholo gy_blog/the-importance-of-positive-feedback-for-young-athletes/

Mojo. (n.d.). The importance of positive feedback. Retrieved from https://www.mojo.sport/ coachs-corner/the-importance-of-positive-feedback

Traceup. (n.d.). Setting goals in sports. Retrieved from https://traceup.com/setting-goals-in-sports

True Sport. (n.d.). How to set goals with youth athletes. Retrieved from https://truesport. org/goal-setting/how-to-set-goals-with-youth-athletes/

Youth Sports Psychology. (n.d.). Setting goals for young athletes. Retrieved from https:// www.youthsportspsychology.com/youth_sports_psychology_blog/setting-goals-for-young-athletes/

Bodybuilding.com. (n.d.). Goal setting! Retrieved from https://www.bodybuilding.com/ fun/a_totw16.htm

Taylor, J. (n.d.). Goal setting for better player performance. Retrieved from https://www. drjimtaylor.com/4.0/goal-setting-for-better-player-performance/

Nord University. (n.d.). Knowledge as the key to success in sports. Retrieved from https:// www.nord.no/en/news-events/news/Pages/Knowledge-as-the-key-to-success-in-sports.aspx

Wikipedia. (n.d.). Knowledge. Retrieved from https://en.wikipedia.org/wiki/Knowledge

Mallick, M. (n.d.). Five advantages to acquire knowledge. Retrieved from https://www. linkedin.com/pulse/five-advantages-acquire-knowledge-mohammad-mallick#:~:text= Knowledge%20helps%20you%20to%20take,than%20knowing%20vocabulary%20and% 20syntax.

Inner Drive. (n.d.). The importance of knowing your role in sports. Retrieved from https:// blog.innerdrive.co.uk/sports/the-importance-of-knowing-your-role-in-sports

Metrifit. (n.d.). Know thyself: The importance of self-knowledge for the modern athlete. Retrieved from https://metrifit.com/blog/know-thyself-the-importance-of-self-knowl edge-for-the-modern-athlete/

Whatfix. (n.d.). The ultimate guide to learning retention. Retrieved June 10, 2023, from https://whatfix.com/blog/learning-retention/

Loma Linda University School of Medicine. (n.d.). Brain-based techniques for retention of information. Retrieved June 10, 2023, from https://medicine.llu.edu/academics/resources/brain-based-techniques-retention-information

TalentLMS. (n.d.). 8 techniques to achieve learning retention in eLearning. Retrieved June 10, 2023, from https://www.talentlms.com/blog/8-tips-techniques-learning-retention/

Olympics. (n.d.). Building a support network. Retrieved June 10, 2023, from https://olympics.com/athlete365/well-being/building-a-support-network/

Soul Cap. (n.d.). Alice Dearing: Every athlete needs a support network. Retrieved June 10, 2023, from https://soulcap.com/blogs/editorial/alice-dearing-every-athlete-needs-a-support-network

Finn's Rec Club. (n.d.). 4 ways parents can support their young athletes. Retrieved June 10, 2023, from https://www.finnsrecclub.com/whatson/4-ways-parents-can-support-their-young-athletes/

Clear, J. (n.d.). The Beginner's Guide to Deliberate Practice. James Clear. Retrieved from https://jamesclear.com/deliberate-practice-theory

Sentio. (n.d.). What is deliberate practice? Sentio. Retrieved from https://sentio.org/what-is-deliberate-practice

Ericsson, K. A., Prietula, M. J., & Cokely, E. T. (2007, July). The Making of an Expert. Harvard Business Review. Retrieved from https://hbr.org/2007/07/the-making-of-an-expert

Inner Drive. (n.d.). What is Deliberate Practice? Inner Drive. Retrieved from https://blog.innerdrive.co.uk/sports/deliberate-practice

Premier Sport Psychology. (2016, December 20). The Importance of Deliberate Practice. Premier Sport Psychology. Retrieved from https://premiersportpsychology.com/2016/12/20/the-importance-of-deliberate-practice/

Transformational Learning Opportunities. (n.d.). Deliberate Practice Strategies. Transformational Learning Opportunities. Retrieved from https://transformationallearningopportunities.com/deliberate-practice-strategies

RescueTime Team. (n.d.). What is deliberate practice? The key to improving in less time. RescueTime Blog. Retrieved from https://blog.rescuetime.com/deliberate-practice/

Metrifit. (n.d.). Optimize your training with deliberate practice. Metrifit. Retrieved from https://metrifit.com/blog/optimize-your-training-with-deliberate-practice/

FS Blog. (n.d.). Deliberate Practice: What It Is and Why You Need It. FS Blog. Retrieved from https://fs.blog/deliberate-practice-guide/

Goodreads. (n.d.). A Quote by Muhammad Ali. Goodreads. Retrieved from https://www.goodreads.com/quotes/72164-i-hated-every-minute-of-training-but-i-said-don-t

Here are the sources you provided, listed in APA format:

1. Opex Fitness. (n.d.). Mindset Training Strategies for Competitive Athletes. Retrieved from https://www.opexfit.com/blog/mindset-training-strategies-competitive-athletes

2. Deep End Fitness. (n.d.). How Athletes Use Mindset Training to Win. Retrieved from https://www.deependfitness.com/journal/how-athletes-use-mindset-training-to-win

3. Success Starts Within. (n.d.). The Difference Between a Training Mindset and a Performing Mindset. Retrieved from https://www.successstartswithin.com/blog/the-difference-between-a-training-mindset-and-a-performing-mindset

Healthdirect. (n.d.). Motivation: How to get started and staying motivated. Retrieved from https://www.healthdirect.gov.au/motivation-how-to-get-started-and-staying-motivated

Ohio University. (n.d.). 6 Tips for Motivating Young Athletes. Retrieved from https://onlinemasters.ohio.edu/blog/6-tips-for-motivating-young-athletes/

NESTA. (n.d.). Strategies and Methods of Improving Motivation for Athletes and Fitness Clients. Retrieved from https://www.nestacertified.com/strategies-and-methods-of-improving-motivation-for-athletes-and-fitness-clients/

STACK. (n.d.). Intrinsic and Extrinsic Motivation for the Youth Athlete. Retrieved from https://www.stack.com/a/intrinsic-and-extrinsic-motivation-for-the-youth-athlete/

KidsHealth. (n.d.). Handling Sports Pressure and Competition. Retrieved from https://kidshealth.org/en/teens/sports-pressure.html

TrueSport. (n.d.). 6 Reasons Athletes Fail to Meet Their Goals. Retrieved from https://truesport.org/goal-setting/6-reasons-athletes-fail-meet-goals/

CinchHQ. (n.d.). How to Determine Goals for Young Athletes. Retrieved from https://cinchhq.com/blog/how-to-determine-goals-for-young-athletes/

Let's Learn Slang. (n.d.). Positive Affirmations for Athletes. Retrieved from https://letslearnslang.com/positive-affirmations-for-athletes/

The Guardian. (2020, November 5). Under Pressure: Why Athletes Choke. Retrieved from https://www.theguardian.com/sport/2020/nov/05/under-pressure-why-athletes-choke

Vision Pursue. (n.d.). Performance Mindset. Retrieved from https://visionpursue.com/performance-mindset/

The Leadership Institute. (2020, February). 3 Ways of Adopting a High-Performance Mindset. Retrieved from https://www.theleadershipinstitute.com.au/2020/02/3-ways-of-adopting-a-high-performance-mindset/

Mini Habits. (n.d.). Growth Mindset vs. Performance Mindset. Retrieved from https://minihabits.com/growth-mindset-vs-performance-mindset/

Conquer Athlete. (n.d.). How Mindset Affects Performance. Retrieved from https://www.conquerathlete.com/blog/how-mindset-affects-performance

TeamSnap. (n.d.). Six Tips for Using Visualization with Young Athletes. Retrieved from https://www.teamsnap.com/blog/coaching/six-tips-for-using-visualization-with-young-athletes

Youth Sports Psychology. (n.d.). Using Visualization to Improve Performance. Retrieved from https://www.youthsportspsychology.com/using-visualization-to-improve-performance/

Success Starts Within. (n.d.). How to Practice Positive Self-Talk as an Athlete. Retrieved from https://www.successstartswithin.com/blog/how-to-practice-positive-self-talk-as-an-athlete

Verywell Fit. (n.d.). Positive Self-Talk. Retrieved from https://www.verywellfit.com/positive-self-talk-3120690

Unity Performance Lab. (n.d.). 6 Focus-Boosting Techniques Used by Elite Athletes. Retrieved from https://unityperformancelab.com/mindset/6-focus-boosting-techniques-used-by-elite-athletes

Entrepreneur. (n.d.). 4 Strategies Used by Superstar Athletes to Become Super Focused. Retrieved from https://www.entrepreneur.com/living/4-strategies-used-by-superstar-athletes-to-become-super/225735

Narbis. (n.d.). Five Surprising Ways to Boost Focus and Athletic Performance, According to Experts. Retrieved from https://www.narbis.com/blog/five-surprising-ways-to-boost-focus-and-athletic-performance-according-to-experts/

Bravo Wellness. (n.d.). The Positive Side of Stress. Retrieved from https://www.bravowell.com/resources/the-positive-side-of-stress

OK Sports and Fitness. (n.d.). The Stressed Athlete. Retrieved from https://www.oksportsand

fitness.com/StressedAthlete.php

News24. (2022, February 15). Athletes Use Stress to Boost Their Wellbeing. Here's How You Can Too. Retrieved from https://www.news24.com/life/wellness/body/condition-centres/stress/athletes-use-stress-to-boost-their-wellbeing-heres-how-you-can-too-20220215-2

Human Kinetics. (n.d.). Pre-Event Nutrition Game Plan. Retrieved from https://us.humankinetics.com/blogs/excerpt/pre-event-nutrition-game-plan

Sports Events Media Group. (n.d.). Tips for Young Athletes. Retrieved from https://sportseventsmediagroup.com/tips-young-athletes/

Coaching Young Athletes. (2021, April 12). 5 Top Tips: How to Best Help a Young Athlete Prepare for a Big Sports Event. Retrieved from https://coachingyoungathletes.com/2021/04/12/5-top-tips-how-to-best-help-a-young-athlete-prepare-for-a-big-sports-event/

Asics. (n.d.). 6 Winning Ways Athletes Mentally Prepare for Competition. Retrieved from https://www.asics.com/us/en-us/blog/6-winning-ways-athletes-mentally-prepare-for-competition.html

KidsHealth. (n.d.). Tips for Sports. Retrieved from https://kidshealth.org/en/teens/tips-sports.html

The Body and Mind Coach. (n.d.). How to Prepare for a Sports Competition. Retrieved from https://www.thebodyandmindcoach.com/how-to-prepare-for-a-sports-competition/

Coaching Young Athletes. (2017, March 2). 6 Tips for Best Competition Preparation. Retrieved from https://coachingyoungathletes.com/2017/03/02/6-tips-for-best-competition-preparation/

Sports Performance Bulletin. (n.d.). How to Prevent Competition Anxiety and Nerves from Getting the Better of You. Retrieved from https://www.sportsperformancebulletin.com/psychology/mental-drills/how-to-prevent-competition-anxiety-and-nerves-from-getting-the-better-of-you

Headspace. (n.d.). 5 Ways to Stay Calm During Competition. Retrieved from https://www.headspace.com/articles/5-ways-stay-calm-competition

World Athletics. (n.d.). Pre-Competition Nerves, Anxiety Advice & Tips. Retrieved from https://worldathletics.org/personal-best/performance/pre-competition-nerves-anxiety-advice-tips

Verywell Mind. (n.d.). Coping with Precompetition Anxiety in Athletes. Retrieved from https://www.verywellmind.com/coping-with-precompetition-anxiety-in-athletes-3024338

Goodreads. (n.d.). Thomas A. Edison Quote. Retrieved from https://www.goodreads.com/quotes/8287-i-have-not-failed-i-ve-just-found-10-000-ways-that

BetterUp. (n.d.). Learning from Failure. Retrieved from https://www.betterup.com/blog/learning-from-failure

Oxford Learning. (n.d.). The Role of Failure in Learning. Retrieved from https://www.oxfordlearning.com/the-role-of-failure-in-learning/

Edutopia. (n.d.). Failure Is Essential to Learning. Retrieved from https://www.edutopia.org/blog/failure-essential-learning-bob-lenz

TeamSnap. (n.d.). How to Talk about Failure with Your Team. Retrieved from https://www.teamsnap.com/blog/coaching/talk-about-failure-team

Athletes Unheard. (n.d.). Here's Why Failure Is the Most Important Skill for Athletes. Retrieved from https://athletesunheard.com/heres-why-failure-is-the-most-important-skill-for-athletes/

HuffPost. (n.d.). 3 Reasons Why Failure Is the Greatest Skill to Learn. Retrieved from https://
www.huffpost.com/entry/3-reasons-why-failure-is-the-greatest-skill-to-
learn_b_58b8b79de4b02eac8876ccc5

Universal Accounting School. (n.d.). How to See Failure as an Opportunity. Retrieved from
https://universalaccountingschool.com/how-to-see-failure-as-an-opportunity/

Harvard Business Review. (2011, April). Strategies for Learning from Failure. Retrieved from
https://hbr.org/2011/04/strategies-for-learning-from-failure

Entrepreneur. (n.d.). Seeing Failure as an Opportunity to Learn From. Retrieved from https://
www.entrepreneur.com/en-ae/growth-strategies/seeing-failure-as-an-opportunity-to-
learn-from-and/308943

Restoic. (n.d.). How to Overcome Failure in Sport, Even When You Feel Like Giving Up.
Retrieved from https://restoic.com/blogs/blog/how-to-overcome-failure-in-sport-even-
when-you-feel-like-giving-up

Entrepreneur. (n.d.). 7 Lessons on Failure You Can Learn from Top Athletes. Retrieved from
https://www.entrepreneur.com/leadership/7-lessons-on-failure-you-can-learn-from-top-
athletes/300699

Sports Strata. (n.d.). How to Embrace Failure in Sports. Retrieved from https://sportstrata.
com/how-to-embrace-failure-in-sports/

Broadview Psychology. (2020, April 21). Resilience: The Ways to Enhance This Critical Skill in
Sports. Retrieved from http://broadviewpsychology.com/2020/04/21/resilience-the-
ways-to-enhance-this-critical-skill-in-sports/

Sport Psychology Today. (n.d.). Resilience and Overcoming Performance Errors. Retrieved
from https://www.sportpsychologytoday.com/sport-psychology-for-athletes/resilience-
and-overcoming-performance-errors/

Mayo Clinic. (n.d.). Resilience: Build skills to endure hardship. Retrieved from https://www.
mayoclinic.org/tests-procedures/resilience-training/in-depth/resilience/art-20046311

Everyday Health. (n.d.). The Ultimate Guide to Becoming More Resilient. Retrieved from
https://www.everydayhealth.com/wellness/resilience/

Up Journey. (n.d.). Real Life Examples of Resilience. Retrieved from https://upjourney.com/
real-life-examples-of-resilience

Webber Nutrition. (n.d.). Goal Setting in Sport. Retrieved from https://webber-nutrition.co.
uk/goal-setting-in-sport/

Army and Navy Academy. (n.d.). Why Setting Goals is Important for Students. Retrieved
from https://www.armyandnavyacademy.org/blog/why-setting-goals-is-important-for-
students/

Success Starts With In. (n.d.). Importance of Goal Setting. Retrieved from https://www.
successstartswithin.com/blog/importance-of-goal-setting

TopResume. (n.d.). 10 Steps to Setting and Reaching Goals at Work. Retrieved from https://
www.topresume.com/career-advice/10-steps-to-setting-and-reaching-goals-at-work

Pativey. (n.d.). The Power of Positivity in Sports. Retrieved from https://pativey.com/the-
power-of-positivity-in-sports/

Verywell Fit. (n.d.). The Impact of Your Attitude and Mood on Your Sports Performance.
Retrieved from https://www.verywellfit.com/attitude-and-sports-performance-3974677

Mayo Clinic. (n.d.). Positive thinking: Stop negative self-talk to reduce stress. Retrieved from
https://www.mayoclinic.org/healthy-lifestyle/stress-management/in-depth/positive-

REFERENCES

thinking/art-20043950

Positive Psychology. (n.d.). Positive Mindset. Retrieved from https://positivepsychology.com/positive-mindset/

Times of India. (n.d.). Importance of having a positive attitude in life. Retrieved from https://timesofindia.indiatimes.com/readersblog/thereality/importance-of-having-a-positive-attitude-in-life-24763/

Stanford Daily. (2011, November 9). The Importance of Teamwork in Sports. Retrieved from https://stanforddaily.com/2011/11/09/the-importance-of-teamwork-in-sports/

Street League. (n.d.). Teamwork and Sports. Retrieved from https://www.streetleague.co.uk/news/teamwork-and-sports

Basketball Manitoba. (2018, March). Teamwork in Sports. Retrieved from https://www.basketballmanitoba.ca/2018/03/teamwork-in-sports.html

Atlassian. (n.d.). The Importance of Teamwork. Retrieved from https://www.atlassian.com/blog/teamwork/the-importance-of-teamwork

Yale University. (n.d.). Why is Teamwork Important. Retrieved from https://your.yale.edu/we-know-teamwork-important-how-important

Bell, R. (n.d.). 17 Famous Examples of Mental Toughness. Retrieved from https://drrobbell.com/17-famous-examples-of-mental-toughness/

TrueSport. (n.d.). How To Teach Mindfulness To Young Athletes. Retrieved from https://truesport.org/performance-anxiety/teach-mindfulness-young-athletes/

KidsHealth. (n.d.). Mindfulness. Retrieved from https://kidshealth.org/en/teens/mindfulness.html

ANZMH. (n.d.). Can Journaling Help with Mental Toughness? Retrieved from https://anzmh.asn.au/blog/mental-health/journaling-help-mental-toughness

Harvard Health Publishing. (n.d.). 4 ways to boost your self-compassion. Retrieved from https://www.health.harvard.edu/mental-health/4-ways-to-boost-your-self-compassion

Positive Psychology. (n.d.). 10 Ways to Practice Self-Compassion. Retrieved from https://positivepsychology.com/how-to-practice-self-compassion/

Think Right Me. (n.d.). 10 Things You Can Do To Get Out Of Your Comfort Zone. Retrieved from https://www.thinkrightme.com/10-things-you-can-do-to-get-out-of-your-comfort-zone/

BetterUp. (n.d.). Why stepping outside your comfort zone is worth it. Retrieved from https://www.betterup.com/blog/comfort-zone

Wikihow. (n.d.). How to Step Out of Your Comfort Zone. Retrieved from https://www.wikihow.com/Step-Out-of-Your-Comfort-Zone

NorthShore University HealthSystem. (n.d.). How to Start a New Routine (and Stick to It). Retrieved from https://www.northshore.org/healthy-you/how-to-start-a-new-routine-and-stick-to-it/

The Spruce. (n.d.). How to Create a Daily Routine. Retrieved from https://www.thespruce.com/how-to-create-a-daily-routine-2648007

Indeed. (n.d.). How to Create a Daily Schedule: Tips and Example. Retrieved from https://www.indeed.com/career-advice/career-development/create-a-daily-schedule

Happify. (n.d.). How to Develop Strong, Meaningful Connections. Retrieved from https://www.happify.com/hd/how-to-develop-strong-meaningful-connections/

Chopra. (n.d.). 10 Ways to Deepen Your Connections With Others. Retrieved from https://chopra.com/articles/10-ways-to-deepen-your-connections-with-others

Oaks Integrated Care. (n.d.). 6 Tips for Forming Meaningful Connections. Retrieved from https://oaksintcare.org/6-tips-for-forming-meaningful-connections/

BetterUp. (n.d.). The Key To Mental Strength Is Not What You Think. Retrieved from https://www.betterup.com/blog/mental-strength

Happify. (n.d.). 5 Ways to Build Lasting Mental Toughness. Retrieved from https://www.happify.com/hd/5-ways-to-build-lasting-mental-toughness/

AZ Quotes. (n.d.). Sports Mental Toughness Quotes. Retrieved from https://www.azquotes.com/quotes/topics/sports-mental-toughness.html